Chas H Dickinson
purchased at
auction from
Z J Bennet
Oct 9th 86

July 30th 18

[*Page* 55.]

"As Clearly Defined in every Particular as if it were Real."

[*Frontispiece.*]

DOWN THE RIVER;

OR,

PRACTICAL LESSONS UNDER THE CODE DUELLO.

BY

AN AMATEUR.

WITH TWELVE FULL PAGE ILLUSTRATIONS BY H. L. STEPHENS.

NEW YORK:
E. J. HALE & SON, PUBLISHERS,
MURRAY STREET.
1874.

LANGE, LITTLE & CO.,
PRINTERS, ELECTROTYPERS AND STEREOTYPERS,
108 TO 114 WOOSTER STREET, N. Y.

GENERAL HENRY L. BENNING,

THIS VOLUME IS DEDICATED,

As a Tribute of Respect,

BY THE AUTHOR.

PREFACE.

THE circumstances which gave birth to the idea of the present work, impelled the writer to great rapidity of execution, not, possibly, unfavorable to the production of some sparks of humor.

On the other hand, constant professional interruptions and business cares have made elaborate revision absolutely impracticable.

Should any of his readers think they recognize herein portraitures of themselves or their friends, he will feel pleasure in such a proof of his capacity for drawing human nature to the life; but he hopes they will extract only amusement from the scenes presented, and be in no wise offended.

In order to the more lively presentment of those scenes, the narrative is placed in the lips of one of the characters portrayed.

THE AUTHOR.

CONTENTS.

APPENDIX.

DOWN THE RIVER;

OR,

PRACTICAL LESSONS UNDER THE CODE DUELLO.

CHAPTER I.

COLONEL HURD EXPLAINS.

I HAVE been induced to write the following history partly by the solicitation of friends, and partly from a desire to inform the public as to the mode of conducting an affair of honor in the most enlightened and modern style.

My own information is limited, but having been thrown in contact with a gentleman of vast experience, many lessons may be learned from a simple recital of facts and conversations occurring during our various interviews, which could never be acquired by ever so careful a reading of "Wilson's Code" and all other published works on dueling.

I enter upon this important work fully impressed with the danger to which I subject myself, and nothing but a sense of duty urges me forward. It will be seen by a careful perusal of this volume, that each word I write on this sublime subject is at the peril of my life. Should the memory of any of the actors in the scenes I shall attempt to portray differ from my own, I may be challenged to mortal combat, and my children perchance left fatherless. It is, therefore, of the utmost importance that every circumstance and conversation should not only be truthfully related, but that it should be done in such a manner as to coincide exactly with the recollections of all the other actors, spectators, and auditors.

The fact that my own views do not concur with those of the greatest duelist of the age, and that I hold that no gentleman should be called out for respectfully stating facts which he believes to be true, even though they should be inaccurately stated, does not in any degree lessen my danger. For any person with whom I may differ in recollection may feel "grieved or pained" by the difference. Nor does my danger cease with the life of the aggrieved, for his relatives and friends might feel it incumbent on themselves to call me to the field. As to whether my male descendants may be held responsible, is a point upon which I have not as yet taken advice.

If any portion of my narrative, therefore, is devoid of romantic interest, I hope my readers will excuse the defect, and not attribute it to the absence of inventive faculties, as it would be inadmissible in a work such as the present to draw upon the resources of the imagination.

CHAPTER II.

LIGHTNING PURSUIT.

LOFTY TO WOODSON.

COLUMBUS, GA., July 18, 11:25 A. M.

To MAJOR JAMES F. WOODSON, Seal, Ala.

I have come from Atlanta with a message of importance requiring personal delivery. Will you kindly meet me here by to-morrow's train at my expense.

Respectfully,

HERCULES D. LOFTY, M. D.

LOFTY TO—789—

COLUMBUS, GA., July 18, 11:26 A. M.

To—789—Atlanta, Ga.

W. not found. Have telegraphed him at Seal, Ala., to meet me here at my expense. Have five men looking for him in this city. I will hunt until I find him.

HERCULES D. LOFTY, M. D.

OPERATOR AT SEAL, TO LOFTY.

SEAL, ALA., July 18, 11:50 A. M.

To HERCULES D. LOFTY, M. D.

Major Woodson not here. Supposed to be in Opelika.

OPERATOR.

LOFTY TO WOODSON.

COLUMBUS, GA., July 18, 11:52 A. M.

To MAJOR J. F. WOODSON, care of COL. G. W. HURD, Opelika, Ala.

I have note of great importance for you. If you are in Opelika await my coming on the 8:30 P. M. train, at my expense. If you are not there let me know where you are.

Respectfully,
HERCULES D. LOFTY, M. D.

LOFTY TO—789—

COLUMBUS, GA., July 18, 11:54 A. M.

To—789—Atlanta, Ga.

W. not at Seal. Have telegraphed to him at Opelika. One of my agents returned, and reports him not in this city.

HERCULES D. LOFTY, M. D.

—789—TO LOFTY.

ATLANTA, GA., July 18, 12 M.

To COL. HERCULES D. LOFTY, Columbus, Ga.

Continue your efforts, and let me know results.

—789—

OPERATOR AT OPELIKA, TO LOFTY.

OPELIKA, ALA., July 18, 1 P. M.

HERCULES D. LOFTY, M. D., Columbus, Ga.

Neither Woodson nor Hurd here: supposed to be in Montgomery.

OPERATOR.

LOFTY TO WOODSON.

COLUMBUS, GA., July 18, 1:02 P. M.

MAJOR JAMES F. WOODSON, Montgomery, Ala.

I am here all the way from Atlanta, with note of vast importance, which must be delivered privately to yourself. Meet me at Opelika by first train, at my expense. If you get this, answer at once.

Respectfully,

HERCULES D. LOFTY, M. D.

OPERATOR AT MONTGOMERY, TO LOFTY.

MONTGOMERY, ALA., July 18, 2 P. M.

To HERCULES D. LOFTY, M. D., Columbus, Ga.

Woodson not here. Supposed to be in Columbus.

OPERATOR.

LOFTY TO—789—

COLUMBUS, GA., July 18, 2:30 P. M.

To—789—Atlanta, Ga.

W. is here. Have seen him. Have spoken to him. Left me abruptly, saying, he would communicate in short time. Find law here against delivery of note. Will have to get him out of the State.

HERCULES D. LOFTY, M. D.

CHAPTER III.

MAJOR WOODSON MEETS COLONEL LOFTY.

On the 18th day of July, in the year of grace 1873, at the hour of 2 P. M., on the east side of Broadway, in the City of Columbus, in the State of Georgia, near the main entrance of the Rankin House, Major James F. Woodson, a resident of Russell County, in the adjacent State of Alabama, suddenly and unexpectedly found himself *vis-a-vis* with a stately stranger, who was in the act of profoundly bowing to him.

This gentleman, after a most courteous salutation, introduced himself as Lofty, and opened a conversation by requesting Major Woodson to walk with him across the bridge which spanned the Chattahoochee River, into the adjoining State, and there receive a note in his possession from Capt. T. J. Porter, a resident of the City of Atlanta, in the State of Georgia, which was of such importance that its contents could not be hinted, or its delivery effected, in any other way than that indicated. The mysterious nature of the request having impressed Major Woodson with the idea that it was unreasonable as well as unusual, taken in connection with the fact that the party making it was entirely unknown to him, prevented a compliance, but he requested his newly-made acquaintance to give his name and address in writing, which was done, after a slight hesitation, upon a slip of paper, in a bold firm hand, as follows:

"Hercules D. Lofty, M. D.
"Mobile, Alabama."

Upon receiving this paper, Major Woodson informed Dr. Lofty that he would, in a short time, communicate with him, and was in the act of turning away, when Dr. Lofty courteously observed, if you propose to walk up the street, I assure you, sir, it will afford me pleasure to walk with you, and improve an acquaintance so pleasantly begun. Major Woodson replied that he contemplated going in an exactly opposite direction (and they parted). Shortly after the termination of this interview between Dr. Lofty and Major Woodson, I was requested by the latter to convey a note to the former, and at 4:30 P. M., of the same day was introduced to Dr. Lofty by my friend, Col. Strong, in the office of the Rankin House.

CHAPTER IV.

HERCULES DIOGENES LOFTY, M. D.—HIS FIGURE, DRESS AND BOW.

HERCULES DIOGENES LOFTY, M. D., I found to be a man about six feet high, of robust frame, and swarthy complexion; his face was cleanly shaven, save an ebony moustache closely trimmed, that joined a small pair of side whiskers corresponding in color, and circular in shape, also closely trimmed. These gave to the contour of his face a resolute military air; aided by the lofty, far-seeing glance of his eagle-eye, his carriage was so erect that his body inclined slightly backwards.

His dress consisted of a large white vest called by merchants "Turkish toweling," densely covered with long nap. This vest was so adjusted upon his person as to show one and three-fourth inches above the collar of his black frock coat. This, with his checked shirt bosom, large neck-tie, and black pants, impressed the observer with the fact that the wearer was a man of pronounced gentility. The address of Dr. Lofty was unusually courteous. He bowed habitually and profoundly. His obeisance inspired even the most inveterate opponents of the *Code* with admiration for its champion. As Col. Strong and myself approached Dr. Lofty he at once recognized Col. Strong, and bowing, expressed great delight at the unexpected meeting. With unfeigned diffidence I attempt the description of the various evolutions necessary to accomplish this bow.

From his erect position, the left hand was brought slowly, with a graceful motion, to the point to which the rim of his beaver would have extended had it been on his head; then his body, from the hip joint upward, inclined forward and downward until nearly parallel with the floor, his face upturned so that his gaze was on the face of Colonel Strong; the left hand, at the same time, being gracefully raised with two fingers and thumb held together, as if supporting his hat; and, simultaneously, the right arm was, by a most graceful waving motion, extended in an almost horizontal position nearly at right angles with his body, and slightly drooping to the floor; the hand extended, with palm to the front, and fingers close together. These evolutions were performed with great deliberation and cautious precision. They required several feet of clear space in front, flank, and rear. They were accompanied by a smile which had gradually changed to a somewhat gloomy expression by the time the bow was complete. No pen can picture the harmony of all these simultaneous movements.

I stood by, astonished and delighted at the great perfection to which a bow could be brought. Colonel Strong bowed slightly and regained his perpendicular before one-third of the descent of Doctor Lofty's bow had been accomplished, and giving him a moment to recover his breath after he had regained his upright position, remarked quietly, "Colonel Hurd, let me make you acquainted with Doctor Lofty."

Thereupon Doctor Lofty commenced a gradual descent into a bow to me, remarking, "Colonel Hurd, it makes me most happy, sir, to form your acquaintance; I feel greatly honored, sir." I felt overwhelmed, and made an utter failure in my attempt to return his bow, as above described. In fact (and I mention it with mortification) a chair was upset in my first effort, and in a second, hurriedly made upon a change of base (just as the frame of the Doctor was "trembling on the rise"), the lower part of my back came so forcibly in contact with the wall as nearly to precipitate me upon the floor. My awkward imitation so discomposed me as to render the interview somewhat constrained.

CHAPTER V.

MAJOR WOODSON'S FIRST NOTE.

Having been introduced to Doctor Lofty as narrated in the last chapter, our conversation was opened as follows:

Hurd. I am requested by Major Woodson to hand you this note (presenting it).

Lofty. Colonel Hurd (bow), it will give me untold pleasure to receive the note you bear from Major Woodson. Will you, sir, do me the courtesy of walking on the veranda; when there I will, with your permission, do myself the honor of receiving it from your hand.

Hurd (with feeble attempt to return the bow). Certainly, sir (and we walked on the veranda where several persons were sitting and lounging).

Lofty (turning to Colonel Strong, who had remained behind). Colonel Strong (bow), will you do us the honor of joining us?

Strong. I will if you desire it (and he joined us).

Lofty. Now, gentlemen (bow), there are two of you here present, I am alone (standing very erect and looking perfectly fearless as his eagle glance, after resting an instant on us, looked far beyond and above us into space). I, therefore, ask leave to call in a witness to the important interview we are about to have during which Colonel Hurd proposes to hand me a note of vital import from Major Woodson. If this favor is granted me (and I might demand it as a right), I will be delighted to receive the important note now in Colonel Hurd's hands.

Strong and myself signifying our assent, Doctor Lofty remarked, "Then, gentlemen (bow), I will retire and bring a witness" (and he retired, returning in a few minutes with Doctor Courtney). By this time many curious eyes were turned upon our party, and I suggested (as soon as Doctor Lofty rose from the bow which he made on his return) that a more private place might be found; "Then," said Doctor Lofty, "gentlemen (bow), will you do me the great honor of walking to my apartment, room No. 7, where I will immediately receive with infinite pleasure the note in Colonel Hurd's hand" (and we went in solemn procession). I, being raised in rural districts, could not restrain myself from a glance behind as we entered the room, and saw the outstretched necks of several waiters and chambermaids, with curiosity depicted on each countenance, and two or three very well dressed gentlemen seemed to be smiling (of course not at us).

Arrived in Lofty's room, I said, "Allow me now, Doctor, to present" (holding out the note)—

Lofty. Pardon me, Colonel Hurd, for interrupting you (bow). You are now my guest, and I hope, sir, you will do me the honor of imbibing with me a little—whiskey—before proceeding with our most important business.

Hurd. Excuse me, Doctor, I never drink whiskey.

Lofty to Strong (bowing). Will you then, Colonel, do me the honor of drinking with me?

Strong (rather stiffly). Not any, thank you.

Lofty to Doctor Courtney. Doctor Courtney, as neither of these gentlemen drink, will you, sir, do me the honor of taking some with me? (and they drank).

Hurd. Doctor, allow me to hand you this note.

Lofty. Colonel Hurd (bow), I will now do myself the honor of receiving the note you bear, but first allow me to remark that it would give me great pleasure if you would take just one drop with me before entering into this important business (bow).

Upon my declining the one drop he touched the note delicately with his finger and thumb by the extreme lower corner, so as to support one half its weight, and said, "I take the liberty of supposing, Colonel, that you are aware of the contents of this note?"

Hurd. I am, sir.

Lofty. Then I call on the gentlemen here present to witness the fact that I, Hercules Diogenes Lofty, now take from the hands of Colonel Hurd this note (taking it). (To me): Colonel Hurd (bow), will you now be so kind as to inform me what it is your pleasure that I shall do with this note.

Hurd. Read it, sir, and answer if you are so disposed, at your convenience. Good evening, sir. And Colonel Strong and myself bowed and moved towards the door.

Lofty. Gentlemen (bow), it will give me much pleasure and honor me greatly if you will be seated and witness my reading of this note. And upon our taking seats he read the note as follows:

"COLUMBUS, Ga., July 18th, 1873.

"HERCULES D. LOFTY, M. D.:

"Sir: will you please inform me of the nature of the communication you have for me?

"Respectfully, J. F. WOODSON."

Lofty. Now, gentlemen (bow), I will detain you but a moment; please do me the kindness to wait and bear my reply to Major Woodson. (We kept our seats and Doctor Lofty sat down to write, when, turning to Doctor Courtney with a bow, he asked:) Doctor, will you do me the honor of consulting your watch; I regard it of the utmost importance to have the exact time.

Dr. Courtney (looking at his watch). It is four and one half minutes after five.

Lofty (turning to me). Colonel, will you oblige me by consulting your pocket time-piece, for, as I remarked, nothing can exceed the importance of having the correct time.

Hurd (looking at his watch). My time is five precisely.

Lofty. I perceive, Colonel, that your time is just four minutes and a half slower than my friend Doctor Courtney; with your permission, Colonel, I shall do myself the honor of adopting your time. I hope, Doctor Courtney, that you do not object (with bow to each of us in turn, and then he wrote his note, and rising with his most courteous bow presented it to me, saying:) Colonel Hurd, will you oblige me by reading that note aloud, and inform me whether you will honor me by delivering it to Major Woodson? (I read it as follows:)

"COLUMBUS, GA.,
"RANKIN HOUSE, Room No. 7—5 P. M.

"MAJOR JAMES F. WOODSON,
"MY DEAR SIR:

"The communication which I hold, I have already had the honor to state to you, personally, is addressed to yourself, and requires a personal delivery.

"You must pardon me if I decline to make any statement concerning it, save to deliver it to yourself.

"I am, dear sir, respectfully, your obedient servant,

"HERCULES D. LOFTY, M. D."

I then assured Doctor Lofty that it would afford me pleasure to comply with his request, and Strong and myself, bowing slightly, withdrew.

After we left the room, Strong was apparently affected with toothache, and placed a handkerchief to his mouth, but soon recovered, and when we had gone some distance smiled.

CHAPTER VI.

PRIVATE DRILLING FOR THE CAMPAIGN.

I CONFESS that I felt chagrined after the interview described in chapters IV. and V. Being country raised, and only having associated with such gentlemen as are produced in the cities of Columbus, Montgomery, and Opelika, it had never been my fortune to associate with a gentleman so courteous and so accomplished in bowing as Doctor Lofty. Feeling acutely that my education in that important accomplishment had been sadly neglected, I determined at once to remedy my deficiency; but how? No gentleman of my acquaintance could give me the necessary instruction; a moment's reflection showed me that I must depend on my own unaided resources. At once a room with a large mirror was procured and a rehearsal commenced. With my first effort the centre-table behind me was overturned, with my second, my right hand was injured by a chair, with the third, my beaver was damaged by a fall. These experiences taught me to reflect, first, that space six feet square at least was necessary; second, that care, coolness, and deliberation were absolutely essential. (Everything in life may be hurried except that bow.) Failure after failure was encountered with manly fortitude, but after hours of ceaseless practice, though aching in every sinew and joint, and especially in my neck, I considered myself passably proficient. But on performing before General Rock, in my best style, his look of astonishment and inquiry made it apparent to my mind that a mistake must have been made by me in some of the details of the bow.

CHAPTER VII.

MAJOR WOODSON'S SECOND NOTE SUCCESSFULLY DELIVERED.

On the eighteenth day of July, at the hour of 8:10 P. M., at the request of Major Woodson, accompanied by Colonel Strong, I bore his reply to Doctor Lofty's last note. We found the Doctor in his apartment, after having learned by a special messenger that he was within and prepared to receive us. On our entrance, Doctor Lofty and Doctor Courtney arose. Doctor Courtney bowed slightly, as was usual among gentlemen with whom I had been formerly acquainted.

Lofty (advancing to centre of room, turned to us). Colonel Hurd, I am delighted to see you. Colonel Strong, you do me great honor in calling upon me (bowing separately to each of us). Colonel Strong made a slight inclination of his head. I stepped four feet in front of him and commenced a regular bow, but Colonel Strong, not being aware of my intention, caused me to be nearly upset by approaching too closely and coming in contact with me when my bow was nearly complete. Hoping, however, that the unfortunate occurrence was not noticed, I said, "Doctor Lofty, allow me to present a note to you from Major Woodson" (presenting it and bowing).

Lofty (resumes, politely ignoring the offered note). Gentlemen (bow), I hope that you will now do me the honor of enjoying my hospitality. Here stands upon this table a fresh bottle of whiskey, and I insist upon your drinking with me. I consider it important, gentlemen, that a drink should be taken, when possible, before entering upon any important business.

Hurd. Excuse me, Doctor, I do not drink whiskey.

Strong. Excuse me, Doctor, I have just eaten supper and never drink after supper.

Lofty. Gentlemen (bow), I hope you will allow me to make a remark: On considering the excuse of Colonel Hurd, I can excuse him, while I, being a most candid man, feel compelled to say that my views do not by any means concur with his on the subject of drinking, and I hope that he will so far reconsider the position which he has taken as to place just two drops of whiskey in a tumbler of water, and go through the form of drinking with me.

Hurd. Not a drop, Doctor, if you will be so kind as to excuse me.

Lofty. Colonel Strong (bow), I excuse Colonel Hurd, because he never drinks; but you, I think, might take a few drops, and although I have just taken a drink, I will do myself the honor of imbibing with you.

Strong. I would prefer not drinking, Doctor.

Courtney. Gentlemen, please take seats (and we did so).

Hurd (rising with pretty fair bow). Doctor Lofty, allow me to hand you this note from Major Woodson.

Lofty (rising). Gentlemen (bow), it is my desire to be excused for one moment from the honor of receiving the note which Colonel Hurd has the kindness to present to me, in order that I may make a remark. Colonel Hurd, will you do me the honor to be seated? (I resumed my seat.) Gentlemen, I was raised by a father who observed all the courtesies and refinements of life. From my earliest infancy he taught me to extend to every guest the hospitalities of my residence. In my early manhood I had the same lesson impressed upon me. My experience in later years has shown me the importance and value of my early education. I have always been considered a most accomplished gentleman, and I esteem it a duty I owe to myself, as well as to my guest, to offer and insist on his taking a drink of whiskey the moment he crosses my threshold, as well as when he departs, and always to keep the bottle convenient for such intermediate drinks as it may suit his pleasure to take, holding myself ready at all times to drink with him.

Strong (rising). Doctor Lofty, I have no recollection of receiving from my father any instruction on the subject of drinking, but have adopted the practice, and have found it at least a prudent one, to drink (if asked) when I wanted whiskey, and when I did not want it to decline.

Lofty. Colonel Strong (profound bow), yours, sir, is true courtesy.

Hurd (rising and moving chairs, etc., to obtain a clear space). Gentlemen (bow almost perfect), I have the honor of bearing a note to Doctor Lofty which I now present. Doctor, will you do me the favor of receiving this note? (presenting it).

Lofty. Colonel Hurd (bow), it affords me the greatest pleasure to receive the note you do me the honor to present (touching the note by the corner with half bow). May I be so bold as to surmise, sir, that you are aware of the contents of this note?

Hurd (with slight bow so as not to displace the note, which he still holds by one corner). Your surmise is correct.

Lofty. Gentlemen (slight bow with wave of left hand), I now call on all of you to witness that I, Hercules Diogenes Lofty, do now freely and voluntarily take this note from the hands of Colonel George W. Hurd. I take it, being ignorant of its contents up to this moment, as a gentleman acting in my position should be at this stage of this most important and interesting proceeding (takes the note, and descends into a most profound bow. On regaining perpendicular): Colonel Hurd, what is your desire that I should do with this note?

Hurd. Doctor Lofty (very fair bow, only slightly impeded by a chair), I hope your kindness will be so much extended as to do me the honor of reading the note, and afterwards take such course as your inclination and great experience shall dictate.

Lofty. Gentlemen (bow), will you permit me to honor myself by complying with the courteous request of Colonel Hurd?

Strong. There is no objection, Doctor; proceed.

Lofty. (First bowing profoundly, reads note as follows:)

"COLUMBUS, GA., July 18, 1873.

"HERCULES D. LOFTY, M. D.

"SIR: As I am compelled to infer from your conversation of to-day, in which you desired me to "cross the river" for the purpose of receiving a message with which you are charged, and also from the tenor of your note of to-day, that your message is a hostile one; and as I am a citizen of, and hold an office in, Alabama, I cannot receive such a communication in that State. I have the pleasure, therefore, to inform you that your communication will be received here in Columbus at such time as it may suit your convenience to communicate the same.

"Very respectfully,

"J. F. Woodson."

After reading this note Doctor Lofty resumed as follows: "Gentlemen, it gives me a sensation of great pleasure to read a note so courteously expressed from a gentleman of such high standing and position as Major Woodson (bow to Colonel Strong and myself). Will you do me the kindness of remaining where you are while my friend Doctor Courtney and myself retire to hold a short consultation? It would give me infinite pleasure if you would, while waiting, divest yourselves of your coats and vests and make yourselves at home in my humble apartment, and, gentlemen (half turn and bow to the table where the bottle stood), if you should on reflection change your minds on the subject of drinking, please do not hesitate to call me, and I will do myself the honor of drinking with you or either of you."

Exit Doctors Lofty and Courtney, with bows, etc.

CHAPTER VIII.

AS TO THE PROCEEDINGS PRECEDING THE PRELIMINARY CORRESPONDENCE IN AN AFFAIR OF HONOR.

ON the return of Doctors Lofty and Courtney, after the private consultation referred to in the last chapter, some conversation between Colonel Strong and Doctor Courtney ensued, and both of them retired from the apartment, leaving Doctor Lofty and myself alone; turning to me, he said, "Colonel Hurd (bow), I propose now to do myself the honor of taking off my coat and vest in your presence, and hope your will kindly consent to do the same."

Hurd. Please excuse me, Doctor, I am so accustomed to wearing my coat that I would not feel equal to the occasion with it off.

Lofty. Colonel Hurd (bow), I accept your excuse as sufficient, and, with your permission, will drink to your health, prosperity and long life, deeply regretting that your (pardon me for saying it) erroneous principles prevent your joining me. (I bowed, he drank, and continued:) I now seat myself to reply to the note which I had the honor of receiving from your hands, but before doing so, Colonel, I wish to call your attention to a portion of this note which has caused me most intense pain and suffering. I was deeply grieved by the same thing in the last note, but supposed the politeness of Major Woodson would cause him to correct the discourtesy. Pardon me for using the word "discourtesy"

(I am a plain, blunt man) in connection with so polished a gentleman as your friend. It is with pain and mortification that I feel myself compelled to call your attention to so unpleasant a circumstance.

Hurd (alarmed, forgetting to bow). Oh, Doctor, to what do you allude?

Lofty. Colonel Hurd (bow, without rising), I will proceed to explain to you my great grief, as well as my wounded feelings will permit. Let me respectfully call to your attention the fact that in my note to Major Woodson, borne by yourself, and written just 5 P. M., I addressed him as Major James F. Woodson. Do you observe that I am addressed by him in these notes (producing Major Woodson's two notes), as Hercules D. Lofty, M. D? It was a terrible wound to me to be so addressed, and a man of your polished and most courteous manners can sympathize with me. I assure you I am always accustomed to be called Colonel. In fact, from my early manhood I have been recognized by that title; and (laying his hand upon his heart) have a better right to it than most men who are so addressed. Never, in all the affairs of honor which I have conducted, have I been addressed by a lower title. I hope, Colonel, you will pardon my candor (bow), but you, notwithstanding your uniform courtesy, have caused me great grief by addressing me as Doctor Lofty.

Hurd (rising, and carefully avoiding chairs, etc., bows). Colonel Lofty, allow me at once to explain and apologize for Major Woodson and myself. Neither of us ever knew you until to-day. Our ignorance on this important subject is owing to the retired life led by both of us. We are merely lawyers, and the great distance which has unfortunately separated us from your place of residence, and our not being in the habit of associating with all of the great men of this age, is our excuse for never heretofore having had the honor of hearing of you. Will you be kind enough, Colonel, to recollect that when Major Woodson had the honor of forming your acquaintance he requested you to write your name and address, and you gave him this slip of paper which reads:

"Hercules D. Lofty, M. D.
"Mobile, Ala."

He followed this direction in addressing you, and no disrespect was intended. In fact, sir, this city has been searched in vain for some gentleman of your acquaintance from Mobile who could give information as to your correct title. A feeling of delicacy alone prevented a personal application to yourself. This error, let me assure you, will not be repeated.

Lofty (rising). Colonel Hurd (bow), say no more. Your apology is accepted. The high respect I have been compelled to entertain for you made me feel confident that some mistake existed on your part, and no intentional disrespect was intended. In order to convince you of my undiminished respect, I will do myself the honor of again drinking to your good health, regretting, as I shall always do, your inability to join me. I take the liberty of expressing again my abhorrence (pardon the word) of any resolution which prevents a gentleman from drinking whiskey (and he bowed and drank, and I bowed). Now, Colonel, I will proceed at once to answer Major Woodson's note. Before doing so, however, allow me to call your attention to a most important matter. I, sir, have had the honor of receiving two notes from Major Woodson; in each of them I find myself addressed as "Sir." You will please remark that I have in my notes addressed Major Woodson as "My Dear Sir." Now, Colonel, you are aware of the vast importance in affairs of honor of having notes properly addressed. In fact, I regard it as next in importance to having the exact and correct time. The simple mention of this will be sufficient, I hope, to cause all future notes from Major Woodson to be properly addressed. I do Major Woodson the justice to suppose that the omission of so important a matter was unintentional.

Hurd. Colonel Lofty (bow), permit me to state that you do Major Woodson great injustice in supposing that the writing of the word "Sir," was unintentional. On the contrary, he intended to write that word and no other. The most expert and polished duelists in this section of the country were consulted before the word was used, and although their opinion should ordinarily weigh little against yours, still, Major Woodson, out of respect to them, having consulted them, feels bound to let the word stand as written, and will, in all future correspondence continue to address you as "Sir."

Lofty. Colonel Hurd (bow), in consideration of these most remarkable circumstances I feel constrained to withdraw my objection. I will not, however, in any future duel allow this precedent to have any weight. I regard this as an exception to the general rule which should govern an affair of honor. Now, Colonel Hurd, I wish your advice on an important point relating to my reply to Major Woodson's note. The question is, shall I again address him as "My Dear Sir," or as "Sir?" By every principle of dueling I should address him as "My

Dear Sir," but considering the remarkable and unprecedented circumstances of this case, Major Woodson being prevented from addressing me as "My Dear Sir," by the advice of friends, who really (pardon me for saying it) know but little about conducting affairs of honor, I am at a loss how to reply; and being convinced, Colonel, that you probably know more about dueling than any man in America, except myself, therefore, in this emergency Hercules D. Lofty asks George W. Hurd to advise him.

Hurd. Colonel Lofty (bow perfect), you do me too much honor, you overwhelm me. Sir, I am but a child compared with you in this noble science. In fact there are gentlemen in this city who are more proficient than myself in the etiquette of dueling. You do yourself great injustice by asking my advice, and it would indeed be indelicate and presumptuous in me to attempt to instruct you. I can only say, if you are pleased to address Major Woodson as "My Dear Sir," it will honor me to bear your note. If, on the contrary, you should address him as "Sir," I will be equally honored by being the bearer.

Lofty. Then, Colonel, I will have to decide the point for myself, and assure you that Hercules D. Lofty has never much difficulty in deciding anything. But let me call your attention to one other point. In neither of the notes that I have had the honor to receive from Major Woodson, are you accredited to me as the bearer. I hope that Major Woodson will do me the honor and yourself the justice to correct this most important defect. I am at a loss to understand how a hostile meeting can be arranged without an observance of this point. This omission I am sure was unintentional.

Hurd. Colonel Lofty (bow), the omission you mention was intentional. After consulting the most experienced duelists and examining all the published works at our command, no case bearing any analogy to this could be found or remembered. It cannot be called "the preliminary correspondence." It seems to precede "the preliminary correspondence." It is a correspondence between a second and a principal, for which we have been unable to find a precedent. I would therefore propose, with deference, however, to your more experienced judgment, to name it "a proceeding preceding the preliminary correspondence in an affair of honor."

Lofty. Colonel Hurd (thoughtful bow without the smile), your suggestion is very forcible, and I shall do myself the honor of agreeing with you as to the name. Although I have conducted many affairs of honor in this way, I still find some preplexing matters in this most courteous note; the polite refusal of Major Woodson to go to Alabama; and the statement that he is willing to receive here the note I bear. May I be so bold, Colonel, as to request your assistance in unraveling this difficulty?

Hurd. Colonel Lofty (bow), I assure you your last note, in connection with your verbal request, equally perplexed Major Woodson. No construction could be placed on your action, except that the note you bore was a peremptory challenge.

Lofty. Colonel Hurd (bow), I cannot see what other construction Major Woodson could place upon it.

Hurd. You will perceive that Major Woodson was bound to presume that you knew the law of the State of your residence.

Lofty. Certainly.

Hurd. He was also bound to presume that you would not do an act unbecoming a gentleman.

Lofty. Certainly, most assuredly.

Hurd. It would be such an act for you to deliver him a hostile note at a point where his reception of it would deprive him of an office, for he would be more damaged by receiving than you would be by delivering it.

Lofty. Certainly.

Hurd. The question then was what could he presume consistently with the presumption that you were acting as a gentleman, which, being beyond all dispute, overrode all other presumptions.

Lofty. Colonel Hurd (without a bow), it is a most remarkable case; what did he presume?

Hurd. Colonel (bow), he presumed that you did not know where he resided, and had never heard of him before.

Lofty. Colonel Hurd (bow, with bland smile, continuing until the bow was nearly complete), Major Woodson did me but justice, and with your permission I will take time to answer his note. Will you do me the honor of calling at 10 P. M., for my answer?

CHAPTER IX.

COLONEL LOFTY'S REPLY, HIS WHISKEY AND HIS EASY-CHAIR.

PRECISELY at thirty-five minutes after nine P. M., Colonel Strong and myself repaired to Colonel Lofty's apartment and found him alone.

Advancing to centre of room, Colonel Lofty bowed and said: "Gentlemen, you do me much honor in calling upon me. Allow me to express my great delight at seeing you. Permit me to call your attention to the fact that there is a fresh bottle of whiskey on the table. I would invite you to drink with me, were it not that I have been twice pained by a refusal; still, gentlemen, if you wish a drink, I will do myself the honor of joining you."

Hurd (bowing). I hope, Colonel, that we have not intruded ourselves before your note was finished, and that we have not inconvenienced you by keeping you waiting.

Strong (slight bow). Colonel Lofty (he had been informed by me as to Colonel Lofty's title), we called by appointment for a note.

Lofty. Gentlemen (bow), I assure you that you need never feel that you intrude upon me. I will feel honored by your coming at any hour, day or night. Please always enter my room without knocking and make yourselves at home. (And turning to me continued—Colonel

Strong having taken a seat unasked, saying that he felt tired:) Colonel Hurd, I will state, that although you come exactly at the moment of time agreed on you do not find me unprepared for your visit. It never takes Hercules D. Lofty long to do anything, and when he says he will have a note written at a certain time, it will be written by or before that time, for Hercules Diogenes Lofty never lies. No, never! In fact, Colonel, my note was completed just seven minutes before you did me the honor of entering my humble apartment, which gave me ample time to take a drink before you came. I never waste time, and therefore nearly always take my whiskey *straight*. I took the liberty of drinking before you came, gentlemen (bow), supposing that you would not join me, but if either of you have changed your minds on this subject (and allow me to hope that you have), I will, as I had the honor to remark upon your entrance, be gratified by imbibing a little more with you.

Strong (without rising or bowing). We only called to get a note, Colonel, and I think it is getting late.

Lofty. I will then, without further ceremony, do myself the honor, Colonel Hurd, of handing you my reply to that most polite note which I received from your hands with so much pleasure (presenting note. I took it delicately by the corner as I had seen Colonel Lofty do when I presented notes to him, and remarked, bowing:)

"Colonel Lofty, may I trouble you by inquiring what it is your desire that I shall do with this note?"

Lofty. Colonel Hurd (bow), it will afford me much pleasure if you will read aloud the letter which I have placed in your hands, and inform me whether or not you will consent to bear it to Major Woodson.

Hurd (bow). It will give me pleasure, Colonel Lofty, to at once comply with your kind request. And I read as follows:

"COLUMBUS, July 18, 1873, 9:28 P. M.
"From Room No. 7, RANKIN HOUSE.

"MAJOR J. F. WOODSON:

"MY DEAR SIR:—Your communication of this date, by the hands of Colonel George W. Hurd, is this moment received——"

Hurd. Colonel Lofty (bow), it is with pain that I mention the fact, but I am compelled by a sense of honor almost as delicate as your own would be under similar circumstances to decline to be the bearer of this note. Allow me, sir (bow), to return it to you (folding and offering to return it).

Lofty. Colonel Hurd, you surprise and pain me beyond measure by your polite refusal to bear this note. I assure you, sir, that I endeavored to express it politely. What can there be in it that you object to? Let me try to correct it.

Hurd. Colonel Lofty (profound bow), it would be unpardonable presumption in me to suggest to so experienced a duelist and polished a gentleman as yourself anything without being forced to do so by your insisting on it.

Lofty. Colonel Hurd (bow), I do insist on it. I assure you no insult was intended, and if you will do me the favor of mentioning your objection I will hasten to correct it.

Hurd. Colonel Lofty (profound bow), it is with reluctance that I mention what to you may seem, at first, a trivial point. I had the honor of being introduced to you by my friend, Colonel Strong. You invited him to join in our first conference, and he has been with me in each visit I have made to you. Neither he nor myself were named in Major Woodson's informal notes as their bearers. Nor do I deem it necessary that either of us should be named in your note as the bearer; yet, sir, I cannot suffer my friend to be ignored and have my own name alone mentioned. Therefore, Colonel, with pain I return you this note.

Lofty. Colonel Hurd (profound bow), you are undoubtedly correct, sir; allow me to say that you have a most delicate sense of honor, which I respect and admire. With your approval I will re-write this note, so as to correct this most egregious error (taking the note).

Hurd. Colonel Lofty (profound bow), I do not know that the error can now be corrected; the shaft has flown, and without the consent of my friend, Colonel Strong, I cannot sanction an amendment.

And we both turned to Colonel Strong, who, to my horror, I saw was sleeping, as quietly as an infant, in a comfortable rocking-chair. As we turned he awoke, and remarked, yawning, and without a bow, "Are not you gentlemen almost through?" And then, without raising his head, he turned his eyes to Colonel Lofty and remarked coolly: "Colonel, I hope you will excuse my nodding (he said nodding, but I felt sure he had been sleeping). You told us to make ourselves at home, and I always nod at home when I have been up the night before." And then to me, "Colonel, I am ready when you are, it is getting late."

Hurd. Colonel Strong, Colonel Lofty and myself were

just discussing a matter of some delicacy concerning you and myself.

Strong. Well, what was it?

Hurd. In this note Colonel Lofty mentions my name but omits yours; he now proposes to write the note over so as to include your name, if you are willing.

Strong. I think, Colonel, it will save time to take it as it is. I do not care about my name being mentioned.

Hurd. Colonel Lofty (bow), as my friend, Colonel Strong, waives the unintentional discourtesy which you did him, I will with your consent continue the reading of your note (and he gave it to me again and I read as follows:)

"I would suggest to you that I can see no reason that would make it more proper for me to deliver the message I bear here than in Alabama. If there should be a reason which would make Georgia preferable to you, I submit that the same thing would cause me to prefer Alabama. However, I will, if you desire, deliver my message to you, either at Chattanooga, Tennessee, or upon the east bank of the Savannah River, in front of the city of Augusta, Georgia, as you may select. I have had the honor to explain to Colonel G. W. Hurd that I did not know anything prevented your reception of the message at the point I indicated first.

"If you will be kind enough to state to me upon what day and at what point you will meet me, I shall have great pleasure in delivering my message.

"I am, dear Sir, very respectfully,

"Your obedient servant,

"HERCULES D. LOFTY, M. D."

Hurd. Colonel Lofty (bow), having now complied with your request, I will feel honored by bearing this note. May I inquire to whom it is your desire that I shall bear it?

Lofty. Colonel Hurd (bow), I will be much honored if you will deliver it in person to your friend Major Woodson.

Hurd. Colonel Lofty (bow), it will afford me much pleasure to do so, and I beg that you will allow me in the meantime to place this note in my pocket.

Lofty. Colonel Hurd, I grant your request with great pleasure. In fact, sir, I consider that in affairs of honor, at this stage of the proceedings, a note may be, with perfect propriety, placed in the pocket of the bearer; in fact it might, under certain circumstances, add to the secrecy absolutely necessary in a matter of such vast importance, and I cannot at this moment see how any offense could be taken, especially when the request is so politely made. (And I put it in my pocket, and called up Colonel Strong, who, to use his own expression, had nodded again.)

Strong. Colonel Lofty, you really must excuse my nodding, I was up nearly all last night, and feel exhausted from loss of sleep.

Hurd. Colonel Lofty (bow), we will now bid you good night, but before doing so will you permit me to consult my watch in your presence?

Lofty. Colonel Hurd (bow), it affords me pleasure to grant your request. As you may have heard me heretofore remark, I consider an accurate observation of time a most important and indispensable necessity in connection with affairs of honor.

Hurd (taking out his watch, examining the time, and

replacing it). Colonel Lofty (bow), I perceive on the examination I have had the honor to make, by your kind permission, that it is now five minutes of eleven P. M. May I be so bold as to inquire whether it would suit your convenience better to receive an answer to this note to-night or in the morning?

Lofty. Colonel Hurd (bow), day or night it is the same to me. Usually I do not retire before one or two A. M. when engaged in affairs of honor, and do not expect to do so before the last-named hour to-night. Certainly not until (a half turn and bow toward the table whereon the bottle stood) I have exhausted my supply of whiskey, and were it not for your prejudices on that subject, which, allow me to say, I never can concur in, I would prefer your returning to-night to participate with me in my agreeable occupation; but as you do not drink, possibly to-morrow would suit you better, and I would suggest the hour of 10:45 A. M. I have plenty of money to pay my expenses. (And all bowing, Colonel Strong and myself retired.)

After making our exit from Colonel Lofty's apartment I asked Colonel Strong what he was laughing at? He said at a dream he had while nodding. I told him that I had been much mortified at finding him asleep on an occasion of such importance, and asked him what his dream was about. He said he had dreamed that Colonel Lofty and myself had bowed to each other and continued to bow and bow until we both happened to bow at the same time, and that our foreheads struck together with a report like a pistol shot, and then he turned suddenly to me and asked what made my forehead so red? I told him that his conduct in going to sleep under such circumstances was enough to bring the blood to the face of his friends, if not to his own. And he said, "Well, 'twas but a dream at the best," and we then and there entered into an agreement that he should never tell his absurd dream.

CHAPTER X.

AN UNEXPLAINABLE INSULT. ANOTHER DUEL ON TAPIS.

ON the morning of the nineteenth, at 8 A. M., I had the pleasure of meeting Colonel Lofty in one of the passages of the hotel. He came forward with a profound bow, grasped my hand cordially, and addressed me thus:

"Colonel Hurd, I am surprised and delighted to find you out at so early an hour. It is quite unusual with me to be astir so early. I generally, after taking my first morning drink at 7 A. M., indulge in a refreshing nap, but on this occasion, finding my bottle empty, have dispensed with my nap in order that I may have it replenished, and feel myself fully compensated for the loss of it by the unexpected pleasure of meeting you. I hope you can spare a few moments of your valuable time that we may have the pleasure of a social conversation, laying aside, as it were, for the moment, that formality it is absolutely necessary we should preserve in our formal meetings. Hercules D. Lofty wants to talk to George W. Hurd."

Hurd. Colonel Lofty (bow), I am entirely at your disposal, and assure you that to me your society is always most agreeable and instructive, and never having had the pleasure of seeing you relax yourself from that stately formality which characterizes Colonel Hercules

D. Lofty, the suggestion you make is doubly acceptable.

Lofty. Colonel Hurd (bow about one-third less profound than usual), while you honor me greatly by your courteous remarks, allow me to say that I think you do me but justice, and to assure you, Colonel, that the regard and admiration you express for me are reciprocated to the utmost extent. Permit me to express the candid opinion, for there is nothing that Hercules D. Lofty so much abhors as flattery, that by the time you arrive at my age you will probably be the most polished gentleman to be found on the face of the globe. I then, in all human probability, will have passed away, not in consequence of the ravages of natural decay, but from the results of old wounds or new ones received upon the field of honor, for Hercules D. Lofty carries his life in one hand, his honor in the other.

Hurd. Colonel Lofty (bow as near the example set by Colonel Lofty, in his last, as possible), you do me too much honor, and but for your distinct disavowal, I would suppose you intended to flatter me, a thing, that like yourself, I utterly detest. Allow me to say that what little polish and courtesy you find in me are due to your example. Who could be otherwise than polite and courteous while in your presence?

Lofty. Colonel Hurd (bow little lower than his last), what you say is ordinarily true, but it pains me to call your attention to the fact that your friend Colonel Strong is not so (pardon me for referring to it) polished and polite as yourself, and I might say that in one instance he treated me (pardon me again, Colonel) almost rudely.

Hurd. Colonel Lofty (bow low, as Colonel Lofty's

last), perhaps I can offer an excuse for my friend. Night before last he did not sleep at all, and his nodding in that luxurious arm-chair, to which, of course, you refer, was unintentional on his part; exhausted nature claimed repose, and he momentarily yielded himself to the tender embraces of Morpheus.

Lofty. Colonel Hurd (two-third bow), your sense of honor is more delicate than that of any gentleman I have ever had the honor to meet, but even without your excuse for your friend, I could well see how any man might fall asleep in that chair. No! I do not complain of that. What pained me so much was of a much graver nature. In fact, I have rarely been more pained and grieved than I was at what must have been (pardon my repeating it) an intentional rudeness on the part of Colonel Strong.

Hurd. To what, Colonel, do you allude? What can my friend have done to give you so much grief? It certainly could not have been intentional.

Lofty. My dear Colonel (bow), I will proceed briefly to explain to you my great grief, to lay bare to you my heart, knowing that a gentleman of your keen sensibility must sympathize with me. Colonel, do you recollect that when you and Colonel Strong first entered my humble apartment, I invited Colonel Strong to drink with me? Now I ask you upon your honor as a gentleman, if you ever saw a drink of whiskey more courteously offered?

Hurd. Colonel Lofty (bow), your courtesy cannot be surpassed, and I must say that in offering a drink to a guest, you, in grace of manner, excel the celebrated Lord Chesterfield.

Lofty (two-third bow). Did you observe, Colonel,

that Colonel Strong, although my offer was so politely made, actually refused to drink? I was wounded to the quick.

Hurd. Colonel Lofty (profound bow), pardon my remarking it, but I hope you will do me the honor to recollect that I at the same time also refused to drink, and if you are offended with my friend, you must also be equally so with me. Allow me then, while expressing my undiminished regard for you, to terminate this interview.

Lofty. Colonel Hurd (profound bow), you do me injustice. Your case stands on a very different footing. You informed me that you never drank, and while disapproving the principles which actuated you, and feeling it my duty so to express myself, I now assure you that no offense was taken in consequence of your refusal.

Hurd. I see, Colonel, that I have unintentionally done you an injustice. Please proceed to explain the wrong you think my friend has done, and perhaps I may be able to account for it to your satisfaction.

Lofty. Colonel Hurd (full bow without the smile), it cannot be accounted for; still I will do myself the honor to explain it, and at least have the consolation of your sympathy. As I remarked, Colonel Strong refused to drink with me when I first asked him, and he did not refuse, in that (pardon me again) polite and courteous manner which you or myself would adopt. I will not mortify you by describing his manner, which we both observed. Again, when I did myself the honor of inviting him to drink a second time, he again refused in a manner—well, I will only say that it was not so courteous as yours. Now, Colonel, soon after you honored me with your first visit, in walking up the principal street in this city, called, I think, Broad Street, I did myself the pleasure of looking into a saloon where I had taken several drinks since my arrival, and what sir, do you think I saw?

Hurd. What?

Lofty. I was horrified by seeing your friend, Colonel Strong, in the very act of raising a tumbler to his lips. I confess that I was so much pained that I turned upon my heel, without even making a remark, or taking a drink myself. Now, Colonel, you see that it is placed beyond all doubt, that Colonel Strong's action can never be satisfactorily accounted for. Hercules D. Lofty knows his duty and dares to do it (standing erect with a most fearless and dignified air). I will be compelled immediately to send a note to Colonel Strong, by an accredited friend, demanding an apology in writing, and if that is refused, blood must flow, to wash clean my honor.

Hurd. Colonel Lofty (bow rather tremulous), allow me to have the honor of saying one word.

Lofty. Colonel Hurd (bow), while nothing you can say can alter my firm resolve, I will do myself the honor of hearing all you can say for your friend.

Hurd. Colonel Lofty (profound bow), I now proceed to do myself the honor of discussing the position you mention. Your grief is occasioned, it seems to me, by two facts. First: That Colonel Strong intended to insult you by his refusal. Second: That his manner distressed you. Do I state the position fairly?

Lofty (bow). You state it most fairly and clearly.

Hurd. Then, sir, I will, with your kind indulgence, explain Colonel Strong's taking the drink you witnessed.

You will please do me the honor to recollect that I informed you that every effort was made by Major Woodson's friends to ascertain your exact and proper title, so as not to do you injustice in addressing notes to you. After all other places of business had been resorted to for that information without success, it was reported that you had been seen entering the saloon you refer to, and several others of like kind; thereupon the friends of Major Woodson dispersed to those places in hopes of obtaining the desired information, and it fell to Colonel Strong's lot to visit the place where you were so pained by seeing him; and while there, simply and alone to prevent the possibility of wounding your feelings, he was compelled to take a drink as an excuse for entering into a conversation with the bar-keeper and others present.

Lofty. Colonel Hurd (bow), we have the honor to be involved in a most intricate and astounding affair of honor, and, Colonel, I am bound to say that your lucid explanation, so far, places Colonel Strong in somewhat better light than I had conceived possible, not being aware of the facts you have mentioned; but allow me to remark, that it is impossible for you to explain the (pardon me) want of courtesy of Colonel Strong.

Hurd. Colonel Lofty (bow), I will do myself the honor of attempting it. Colonel Strong, as you are probably aware, is a scion of one of the first and most distinguished families of North Carolina. You are not from that State, I believe, Colonel?

Lofty. No, sir.

Hurd. Then permit me to refer to a peculiarity well known to us about the scions of such families. They are, pardon me, you know, just a little careless about the details of etiquette and courtesy, which you and myself admire so much, acting, I suppose, on the supposition that every one knows them to be gentlemen.

Lofty. Colonel Hurd (bow), I am aware of the peculiarity to which you refer, but feel it due to myself to say, that where one of those gentlemen associates with Hercules Diogenes Lofty, the peculiarities of States and of families must give way. Hercules Diogenes Lofty must be treated by those rules of politeness which he recognizes, and Colonel Strong must either apologize in writing or meet me on the "field of honor." I must insist either on blood, or an apology.

Hurd. Colonel Lofty (bow), only to prevent the flow of blood would I be so bold as to make a suggestion to you; but, feeling it to be my duty, I suggest respectfully that an informal note might answer every purpose, and Colonel Strong might possibly explain to your satisfaction.

Lofty. Colonel Hurd (bow), while I, like yourself, always wish to avoid a flow of blood, yet, in this instance, I feel bound by every principle of honor to act in the manner first indicated by me. For any man to decline to drink with Hercules D. Lofty, except (bow) when the gentleman declining never drinks, is a wound to my honor which must be redressed under the code. May I be so bold, Colonel, as to inquire how you think Colonel Strong will answer the note I intend to send him? It is a matter of the utmost indifference to me, and I merely ask your opinion as an act of courtesy to yourself.

Hurd. Colonel Lofty (bow), you overpower me by your politeness. Your question, however, is by no means easy to answer; much depends upon the humor

Colonel Strong is in when your friend delivers your note. If it should be immediately after he has read some pleasant and well-deserved compliment to one of his editorials, or in a genial mood, he may answer your note in a very kind and conciliatory manner. If, on the contrary, your friend finds him in a bad humor, which, by the way, is most probable—say just after correcting a bad piece of proof—his answer would, in all probability, be anything but conciliatory.

Lofty. Colonel Hurd (bow), I feel under deep and lasting gratitude for your views on this most important subject, and for your sympathy in my great grief. But it is to me perfectly immaterial what course Colonel Strong may see fit to pursue on the reception of my note. With your permission I will remark, that when I had the honor to meet you I was on my way to the barroom under this hotel, designing when there to imbibe a little whiskey ; and, but for those principles of yours, of which I cannot, with courtesy to yourself, express my full abhorrence, which forbid your drinking, we might, during this most interesting conversation, have taken several drinks.

Hurd. Colonel Lofty (bow), please excuse me for having detained you so long. I really never know how to tear myself away from your pleasant society (and we bowed and parted).

CHAPTER XI.

THE MIDNIGHT DUEL.

My next interview with Colonel Lofty was an informal one, in his apartment, at 9:42 A. M.

After a most courteous reception, in the urbane and dignified manner for which the Colonel is so distinguished, I introduced the conversation as follows:

Hurd. Colonel Lofty (two-third bow), the place which Major Woodson is inclined to select, at which to do himself the honor of receiving the important note you bear, is Neil's Landing, in Florida; I mention this fact informally, to ascertain whether you have any objection to that point. If the place designated does not suit you, some other will be named.

Lofty. Colonel Hurd (two-third bow), no place could be mentioned which would suit me better. And permit me to say, that your delicate manner of intimating the fact before making a formal announcement, does both you and myself great honor; excels any practice under the code that I have ever witnessed, except in some of the affairs which I have had the honor heretofore to conduct myself. I suppose, Colonel, that you always keep the code near you.

Hurd. Colonel Lofty (two-third bow), I always have it with me, and since I have been honored by making your acquaintance, sleep with it under my head.

"It is the most beautiful Ceremony I ever witnessed."

[*Page* 55]

Lofty. Colonel Hurd (two-third bow), I have long since adopted that practice myself, and find it adds to the clearness of my thoughts. Often in the still, small hours of the night, the vision of a most interesting duel is presented before my mind's eye, as clearly defined in every particular as if it were real. Observe how much worn my code is, Colonel, just above you on the mantlepiece—allow me to show it to you (and he handed it to me).

Hurd. Colonel Lofty (two-third bow), with your permission I will read it (and obtaining the permission asked, read it* and then remarked): Colonel, this code which I have the honor of receiving from your hands, is one which I have never heretofore had the pleasure of seeing; I perceive it is "thirty-six commandments" issued by the fire-eaters of Ireland in 1777, and adopted by the Knights of Tara.

Lofty. Colonel Hurd (two-third bow), you astonish me, by the statement that you never heard of this world-renowned code of honor. Why, sir, many years ago, the opponents of our noble profession attempted to burlesque this code upon the stage, but the effort did not succeed. You will notice that under it when a gentleman apologizes for certain offenses, he has to do so on bended knees, presenting a cane to his antagonist with which to flog him. It is the most beautiful ceremony I ever witnessed. I am indeed surprised, that a gentleman so remarkably polished, and educated in dueling as yourself, should not have heard of it.

Hurd. Colonel (bow), you do me injustice. I hope you will do me the honor of recollecting that I did not express myself as ignorant of the existence or contents of

* For copy of the Irish code, see Appendix.

this remarkable code; but that my remark was, that I had never had the pleasure of "seeing" it. I have "heard" of it from my "earliest infancy."

Lofty. Colonel Hurd (profound bow), allow me to apologize for my unintentional misinterpretation of your words. It astonished me to think that you had never heard of this most superb code of honor. I am not so much surprised at your never having seen it, as there are only a few copies of it in the world. May I be so bold, Colonel, as to inquire what code you refer to as having always with you?

Hurd. Colonel Lofty (bow), you gratify me by making the inquiry. The code which I study by night and by day, when not enjoying your most delightful society, is John Lyde Wilson's.

Lofty. Colonel Hurd (bow), it strikes me, sir, that I have heard of Wilson's Code; will you do me the honor of allowing me to see it, if convenient? (I handed it to him, and he proceeded to read it.*)

Hurd. Colonel Lofty (bow), may I trouble you by asking permission to sit while you read? The breeze coming in from that western window is so pleasant that I wish to sit near it.

Lofty. Colonel Hurd (bow), you will oblige me by doing so. And we both bowed; and I seated myself near the window. After reading the code, Colonel Lofty arose, and bowing profoundly, remarked: "Colonel, I see one or two pretty good points in this code, which I have had the pleasure of reading."

Hurd. Colonel Lofty (bow), it would be presumption in me to advocate any code of honor, which a gentleman of your great and unexampled experience had

---

* See Appendix.

not practiced under. It is true, that the most experienced duelists and cultivated gentlemen in this section of the country admire and sustain Wilson's Code. The argument they use is, that as civilization and refinement progress, all arts and sciences progress with equal steps; and they think that the science of dueling is, by Wilson's Code, placed upon a true basis. I would, however, like to hear your views upon this important point before my own mind is made up.

Lofty. Colonel Hurd (bow), since refreshing my mind, I recollect having conducted several affairs under this code. As I had the honor of mentioning to you, there are several passably good points in it, and sir, with your permission, I will do Mr. Wilson the honor of adopting his code in the present important and most interesting affair, by no means, however, making it a precedent in any future affairs I may have the pleasure of being connected with; for Colonel Wilson was, at the time he wrote, far behind this age in this noble science.

Hurd. Colonel Lofty (profound bow), there are, sir, two insurmountable objections to my accepting your most generous proposition. First, I am not, and cannot be, the second of Major Woodson, on account of my near relationship to him. Second, I can, by no process of reasoning, see how this intricate affair can now be made to conform to Wilson's Code.

Lofty. Colonel Hurd (bow), your first objection, I will do myself the honor to say, is well taken; but your second, I confess, astonishes me. Will you be so kind as to explain further?

Hurd. Colonel Lofty (bow), I will at once comply with your request. Mr. Wilson lays it down as a rule, that a hostile message should not be sent in the first instance. Now in this remarkable case, you propose to send a hostile message in the first instance; the difference seems to me to be irreconcilable. But I pause—with deference to your better judgment.

Lofty. Colonel Hurd (bow), Mr. Wilson showed that he knew nothing about what he was writing when he wrote that section. I do myself the honor to say that he was mistaken, and my own experience proves it. Why, sir, just thirteen years ago to-night, I was attending an opera with a lady in the city of Brooklyn, when a gentleman grossly insulted her. I, of course, took no notice of the insult at the time, but as soon as I had deposited the lady at her residence, I went in search of the gentleman who had insulted her, and after looking for him in several bar-rooms, I at last found him in one, at 12:15 A. M., just in the act of raising a glass of whiskey to his lips. I touched him lightly on the back, and he placed his glass upon the counter without drinking, and called for another glass for me; thereupon we drank together, and when he had settled for the drinks, I simply nodded towards the door; he, of course, understood me, and we entered my buggy which was standing near. I had in it a case of flint and steel dueling-pistols, and two bottles of very fine whiskey. The night was so pitch dark, it was impossible to see a hand within six inches of your face. We drove several miles out of the city, into an old field used for making brick, and arrived at 1:25 A. M. When there, we stepped off the ground, measuring only twelve paces on account of the inky darkness of the night. Our terms of combat were, that we should exchange pistols after every shot, and continue the combat until one or both were killed. At the first fire my pistol flashed in the pan, and my adversary's ball passed through my right lung. We then, of course, exchanged weapons, and took several drinks together, re-loaded, and prepared for another exchange of shots. My adversary having the pistol which had failed to fire, in re-priming it, adopted the plan of pouring into the pan, first powder, and then whiskey, and then powder and whiskey again. At the signal to fire, I waited until he pulled his trigger, when, as I expected, the whiskey and powder ignited, illuminating his face with the blue blaze. I fired instantly, my ball passing through his brain, entering a quarter of an inch above his right eye; he only lived long enough to request me to take his watch and pocket-book from his person, and deliver them to his wife. I took them by the light of the blue flame, which was still burning, and would have disposed of them as he requested, but for the fact that next morning the papers were full of what they were pleased to call a brutal murder and robbery, and I have been compelled to keep them, much against my will, up to this time. But to the point. My antagonist and myself, before he died, agreed to consider that duel as in substantial conformity with Wilson's Code. But admitting that Colonel Wilson might be correct in the section you refer to, no living man knows what the contents of this note, which I keep so sacredly guarded, are, except Captain Porter and myself.

Major Woodson, I admit, has a right to presume it hostile, and, it may be, is compelled to do so from the correspondence; but, Colonel, let us suppose that Major Woodson should be mistaken in his presumption (but please do not understand me as admitting the possibility of such a thing); then might not this intricate affair be brought under the Wilson Code?

Hurd. Colonel Lofty (profound bow), your reasoning, sir, is perfect, and the precedent you have so modestly referred to is overwhelming; but still, not being Major Woodson's second, I do not feel authorized to make the arrangement you so magnanimously propose.

At this interesting stage of our conversation, a policeman made his appearance at the door, and, about the same time, Dr. Courtney entered through the French window, and said, hurriedly: "Gentlemen, the police force are upon you," and, passing on to the door, obtained from the accommodating policeman a five minutes' respite, when Colonel Lofty, turning to me, said, after a profound bow: "Colonel Hurd, in this most interesting state of affairs, which nearly always occurs in the affairs of honor which I have heretofore had the pleasure of conducting, I will first do you and myself the honor of taking a drink (and he drank). By acting in this manner, at this important crisis, any skulking policeman who happens to be passing the window, will see that we are perfectly cool and collected. I will now, Colonel, by your kind permission, place this bottle in my pocket, to provide for such casual refreshment as I may need during the interval of my retirement (and he bowed as usual, with the bottle in his left hand, and, as he regained his perpendicular, placed it in his right coat-tail pocket). I will now proceed in a leisurely and dignified manner, to place myself out of reach of these prying and meddlesome policemen, who are the bane of my life. I hope you will be able to take care of yourself, Colonel. Allow me now to bid you good morning." As he bowed before retiring, the neck and one-third of

"Allow me now to bid you Good Morning." [*Page* 60.]

the bottle projecting from his pocket stood upright, and he retired through the window.

Being left alone, I went quietly to my room, and was shortly afterwards arrested, and carried before Judge Williams. No proof being made against me, and my manner (owing to my recent association with Colonel Lofty) being remarkably urbane and courteous, his honor ordered and adjudged me to be a perfectly harmless individual, and suffered me to depart in the full enjoyment of the boon of liberty, so precious to the American citizen. My friend, Colonel Strong, however, who was also arrested, was not so fortunate, though more innocent; he was placed under a heavy bond, conditioned to keep at peace while in the State of Georgia.

CHAPTER XII.

A CONFLICT BETWEEN THE CODE OF HONOR AND THE CIVIL CODE.

In the afternoon of the 19th of July, when the excitement of the people had subsided, and the minions of the law were satisfied that no duel was afloat (except one in which Colonel Strong was supposed to be engaged, with a man whom he had never seen), all eyes being turned upon my unfortunate friend, who was considered to be a person desirous of disturbing the peace of the State of Georgia, in my usual meek and quiet manner; I wended my way to Colonel Lofty's apartment, who welcomed me in his own remarkably polite manner, but his deportment, I thought, seemed rather subdued, so much so, that I considered it my duty to inquire if any misfortune had befallen him. With that courtesy, which no calamity could overcome, he replied: "My dear Colonel Hurd (bow), a most serious misfortune did befall me since I had the pain of parting from you. You will do me the honor to recollect, that at the moment of our parting, under the most exciting set of circumstances, surrounded as we were by the whole police force of this city, under such circumstances as would deprive most men of all power of calm and deliberate judgment, I had the remarkable coolness and foresight to place in my pocket a bottle of whiskey. I had done myself the pleasure of taking but one drink out of that bottle (which you did me the honor to observe). Well, sir, just before reaching my place of concealment, which had been selected beforehand, with my usual precaution in these delicate affairs, I had the misfortune to meet a stranger, and thought it but courteous to salute him; and, in making a polite bow, my bottle was, by some unaccountable means, precipitated from my pocket, and broken in fragments. Colonel, I assure you, it was the best whiskey in the city; and, sir, I was forced to remain in my place of concealment for two hours and five minutes before I could procure a drink."

Hurd. Colonel Lofty (bow), it must have been a terrible affliction; let me assure you of my sympathy; had it not been for this untimely interference of the police, your whiskey would have been at this time safe, with but little danger of breaking the vessel which contained it.

Lofty. My dear Colonel (bow), you are undoubtedly correct, the whole fault lies with the officers of the law; who, I must say, are always meddling with affairs which do not concern them; they seem to take a special delight in interfering with quiet, peaceable gentlemen. In olden times such interference was not tolerated, sir! The gentlemen of this country should combine, and frown them down. Would you believe it, sir, I, Hercules D. Lofty, am, at this moment, under a bond to keep the peace in this State.

Hurd. Colonel Lofty (bow), your statement surprises me! A gentleman so courteous as yourself, placed under a bond to keep the peace!

Lofty. Colonel Hurd (bow), it is true, sir, and absolutely without any just cause. I had challenged a man (whom I, at the time, mistook for a gentleman) because he grossly insulted me, by refusing to return my bow when I was introduced to him, and he, refusing to apologize, or meet me on the field of honor, I was compelled, by every principle of honor, to degrade him. Well, sir, I merely did my duty, in the mildest and most quiet manner possible. After first giving him notice that I felt myself compelled to degrade him, on the first occasion I should have the pleasure to meet him, I walked quietly into his store, took him by the right ear, led him by it to the front door, and, when there, I *quietly and peaceably* kicked him out into the street. Upon my honor, sir! I disturbed no one! The facts I have mentioned are absolutely *all I did,* except to mention to him, *privately* (in the presence of some eight or ten persons, who had assembled upon my acting as I have stated), that the next time I met him I should feel compelled to wring his nose. Now, for merely doing my duty, in this *mild* and temperate manner (and you well know that a gentleman could do no less under such circumstances),. I was bound over, sir — yes, Hercules D. Lofty was actually bound over to keep the peace!! I submit to you, Colonel Hurd, whether it was not an act of great injustice?

Hurd. Colonel Lofty (profound bow), your statements present a most interesting case. It seems, from your recital of the facts, that you did not intend to violate the peace of the State, and were merely acting under a sense of the duty you owed yourself, and the gentlemen of the country whom you are so eminently qualified to represent.

Lofty. Colonel Hurd (bow), I see you appreciate my position exactly.

Hurd. Colonel Lofty (bow), the laws of our country rarely punish a man (even for a most flagrant breach of the peace) when a criminal intent is wanting.

Lofty. Exactly, Colonel, that is the very position I take. I see, sir, that you have acquired a complete mastery of the miserable farce, (pardon me), called law, as well as of the noble science of dueling.

Hurd. Colonel Lofty (bow), you do me too much honor. But I was going on to remark, that there are certain presumptions which are indulged in by the law. One of them is, that a man is presumed to intend the result which will necessarily follow his act, and if this presumption was indulged in very strongly by the judge who tried your case, I can see how he might, by this technicality, bind you over to keep the peace, and still be within the pale of the law. Of course, I would not have you to suppose that I could defend his position on any moral ground.

Lofty. Colonel Hurd (bow), you may be right; but, sir, the idea of a gentleman being bound over to keep the peace upon a mere technicality!

Hurd. Colonel Lofty (bow), it is, indeed, lamentable. But I intrude upon your valuable time. Permit me to do myself the honor of placing in your hands this note of Major Woodson.

Thereupon we went through all the necessary ceremonies of delivering a note, which have been hereinbefore detailed, and the note was, finally, duly read, as follows:

"RANKIN HOUSE, COLUMBUS, GEORGIA, July 19, 1873.

"COLONEL HERCULES D. LOFTY:

"SIR:—It will suit my convenience to receive any communication to me, with which you are charged, at

Neil's Landing, in Florida, on the Chattahoochee River. I am informed that boats leave here for that point on Tuesdays and Thursdays. Please be so kind as to indicate the time at which it will best suit you to repair to that place.

"Very respectfully,

"J. F. WOODSON."

Lofty. Colonel Hurd (profound bow), I will at once do myself the honor of replying to this most courteous note; but before doing so, I will remark, that I would be greatly delighted if you would be so kind as to lend me, for the space of twelve hours and thirty minutes, that most remarkable code of Mr. Wilson's. After the most careful thought and reflection, I have concluded to do Mr. Wilson the honor of having five hundred copies of his code printed, for general distribution throughout the length and breadth of this great country. I do not expect, sir, to realize one cent from this undertaking. I wish to do it merely for my country's good. Every male child in this broad land should have a copy of Wilson's Code placed in his hand at least by the time he reaches the age of ten years, and it should be made his daily study, from that time onward, until his death. Colonel, I propose further, to present to yourself, in token of the great regard and respect I have for you, thirteen copies of this code, for general distribution among your friends. Let us join together and educate the masses in this noble science.

Hurd. Colonel Lofty (profound bow), allow me to say, that the heartfelt interest you take in the future of our country, does you much honor; and while I confess that parting from my code, for twelve hours and thirty minutes, will be a great privation to me, still, following your noble example, when you voluntarily deprived yourself of your whiskey, by an act of mere courtesy to a stranger, I will yield to your flattering request; feeling myself more than compensated and greatly honored by your offer of thirteen copies. But, allow me to suggest, that you have also printed at the head of the code, these words: "Endorsed and approved by Colonel Hercules Diogenes Lofty."

Lofty. Colonel Hurd (profound bow), your last remark shows that you appreciate my position. But I do not know that Hercules D. Lofty will endorse in every particular this code. I may, at some future time, see fit to give a qualified approval of it.

Hurd. Colonel Lofty (profound bow), while I regret that you do not take my suggestion, it is more than probable your views are correct. But I detain you from replying to the note of Major Woodson. Will you permit me to occupy this rocking-chair while you write?

Lofty. Colonel Hurd (bow), you will greatly honor me by taking it. And now I will at once proceed to answer this most polite note; but first, Colonel, I will, with your permission, take a drink, always lamenting, as I do, that your principles (I will say no more, lest I offend you) prevent your joining me. Ah, Colonel, how much enjoyment I have missed by your misfortune in not knowing the pleasure of drinking! It gives zest and refinement to an affair of honor. In fact, I have never seen one carried on successfully without it.

He bowed, and drank; I bowed, and sat down; and Colonel Lofty proceeded to write his note.

After it was completed he, in due form, handed it to

me, with the usual ceremony, so important in such an affair. And the note was read as follows:

"COLUMBUS, July 19, 1873.
"At RANKIN HOUSE, Room No. 7, 5 P.M.

"MAJOR J. F. WOODSON, *present en ville.*

"I have the honor to acknowledge your note of this instant, handed me by Colonel G. W. Hurd. In reply, I will say, that Neil's Landing, in Florida, upon the Chattahoochee River, will suit me very well, and, also, I would say, that I will take the Tuesday's boat.

"I am, sir, with profound respect,
"Your very obedient servant,
"HERCULES D. LOFTY, M. D."

CHAPTER XIII.

PREPARATIONS FOR DEPARTURE.

At 6 P. M. of the 29th day of July, 1873, the note of Colonel Lofty, dated 5 P. M., was delivered by me to Major Woodson.

All was now bustle and confusion among the Major's friends. While preparations for departure on Tuesday's boat were being rapidly made, wills were executed, seconds, surgeons, and surgical instruments sought for, etc.; everything was done in the most mysterious and secret manner; only tried and true friends could be trusted.

Meantime the party of Colonel Lofty were equally active and equally prudent. Messages flashed over the wires by night and by day. On Sunday afternoon Captain T. J. Porter and Major John F. Shelton had joined Colonel Lofty at the Rankin House, bringing with them arms and ammunition.

By Monday morning, July 21st, all this prudence on the part of all parties had gradually excited the curiosity and alarm of the good citizens of Columbus to an unnatural pitch. Mothers kept their children in-doors; respectable heads of families consulted together as to the best means to prevent the flow of blood.

A Board of Honor was organized, and intervened to prevent a hostile meeting, if possible, under the code.

They addressed a polite note to each party, asking that they might be allowed to search diligently into the origin of the misunderstanding, with a view to ascertain whether some misapprehension or mistake did not exist, which might be corrected, and harmony restored. This was responded to favorably by Colonel Lofty and a gentleman who was authorized to act for Major Woodson. I am unable to give a copy of Major Woodson's reply, as written by his friend. Colonel Lofty, however, in this instance, overcoming his native modesty, allowed two notes, written by himself, together with one from the Board of Honor, to be printed in the "Herald," thereby enabling me to obtain copies of them, which I set out *verbatim*.

"COLUMBUS, July 21, 1873.
"RANKIN HOUSE, Room No. 7, 11 A. M.

"COLONEL CHARLES M. POTTS, W. T. LUMKIN, Esq., COLONEL JOHN M. BUFORD, *present en ville.*

"GENTLEMEN:—Your favor of this A. M., addressed to Captain T. J. Porter and Major J. F. Woodson in duplicate, and handed to me for delivery to Captain T. J. Porter, claims a reply from me. I have the honor to state to you, that up to this moment no communication of any character has taken place between Captain Porter and Major Woodson.

"I will frankly own to you, that I am the bearer of an undelivered message from Captain Porter to Major Woodson.

"I will state, that some correspondence has passed between Major Woodson and myself, relative to the point at which my message should be delivered. I will also own, that an agreement as to the point of delivery has been reached by us. I will say to you, gentlemen, that I so highly appreciate the lofty and chivalric spirit, which has moved you to address this letter to which I am replying, that I will frankly, as you desire, consent to the mutual and temporary withdrawal of all the correspondence which has passed between Major Woodson and myself.

"I permit the withdrawal for the space of twelve hours and ten minutes, with the understanding that, should your humane effort prove of no avail, that affairs between Major Woodson and myself resume their present position, and that I shall repair to the point we agreed upon at the time we have appointed. At the proper time, and at your request, I have no objection to submit to you the message with which I am charged.

"I am, gentlemen, with profound respect,
"Your very obedient servant,
"HERCULES D. LOFTY, M. D."

To this note of Colonel Lofty, the Board of Honor replied as follows:

"COLUMBUS, GA., July 21, 1873.

"COLONEL H. D. LOFTY:

"Your reply of this instant received, together with a similar one from General Pearson, on behalf of Major Woodson; and now, in pursuance of a purpose so honorably seconded by each of you, we respectfully ask that you submit to us the cause of complaint in the premises, to the end that the same may be considered, and further action on our part taken, which we hope may be the means of an amicable adjustment between the gentlemen.

"Respectfully,
"Your obedient servants,
"CHARLES M. POTTS,
"W. T. LUMKIN,
"JNO. M. BUFORD."

Colonel Lofty's reply to this note was as follows:

"COLUMBUS, GA., July 21, 1873.
"RANKIN HOUSE, Room No. 7, 1:25 P. M.

"COLONEL CHARLES M. POTTS, W. T. LUMKIN, Esq., COLONEL JNO. M. BUFORD, *present en ville.*

"GENTLEMEN:—Your second note of this date is just received; in reply, I have the honor to refer the cause of complaint upon the part of my friend.

"The copy of 'The Sun' which I inclose, contains an article signed by Major Woodson, in which he refers to Thos. K. Smith, now deceased, who was a fourth cousin of Captain Porter, and in which article Major Woodson states, among other things, that Thomas K. Smith, deceased, did, in his lifetime, have criminal connection with one Caroline Myers, and that said Thomas K. Smith was not at the time of his death a member of any church.

"An unqualified retraction of every statement in this article, so far as the same relates to Captain Porter's relation, is all that is desired.

"I am, very respectfully,
"Your obedient servant,
"HERCULES D. LOFTY, M. D."

Whatever doubt may have heretofore existed as to

the propriety of making public any action resulting from an unsuccessful intervention of a self-constituted Board of Honor, is now set at rest by the high authority of this precedent, set by the distinguished Colonel Lofty, in allowing this correspondence to be printed. Upon the intervention of the Board of Honor, the wires were again called into requisition.

Dispatches flashed with lightning speed to Seal and Opelika, to which points Major Woodson and myself had returned to hastily wind up our earthly affairs. Post-horses and steam were put into active use to bring us to Columbus in view of a reconciliation. The people became more quiet; scorn and contempt were depicted on the faces of many, and bets were freely given and taken, that one or other of the combatants would (using a vulgar expression) "take water." (Colonel Lofty was never known to take it.)

The vigilance of the police was relaxed. Many thought and expressed themselves (in the unrefined parlance in vogue at the time), that the thing (so they called an affair of honor) was "squashed," or had "busted."

The efforts of the Board to reconcile matters being fruitless, they ceased their labors at 1 A. M., on Tuesday morning. The police force were reported to have sniffed the failure to adjust, and were on the alert at daylight, but the good citizens slept quietly in their beds, until they were aroused by the astounding report that Colonel Lofty, Captain Porter, and Major Shelton had escaped the vigilance of the police, and had been seen driving out of the city at 3 A. M., with furious speed, in a carriage accompanied by outriders.

The whereabouts of Major Woodson and myself were

not apparently suspected, except by friends. The boat was to leave at 8 A. M. Major Woodson and myself, a short time before that hour, after taking a final farewell of many true friends, who did not know that they would ever see him in life again, especially, of that brave boy who, with a smile on his lip, and almost a tear in his eye, said, "Just keep cool, and shoot as you did at the pigeons, and we will see you safe home again, Uncle James."

We wended our way by quiet back streets, and as we went, the boy's words rang in my ears and I said, "Major, that boy will make a man; he's game;" and then I regretted my remark, for I saw in the eye of the veteran of two wars a moisture unusual to those clear orbs, for he loved that fatherless boy; but he only said, "Yes, he'll do pretty well, the conceited puppy, giving me advice."

As we neared the landing, a friend met us with the information that the police force of the city were guarding every avenue to the boat; then the Major's eyes flashed fire, and he said, "He'd fight his way through." I paused for a moment to consider what Colonel Lofty would do, were he surrounded by such adverse circumstances. Well, thought I, first, he would take a drink, but in a moment the thought, quicker than lightning, flashed through my mind of the gallant manner in which the Colonel and his party had dashed out of town. I had it. A horse and buggy, and we could charge through a regiment of policemen. Back from the river we darted two blocks; Major Woodson was secreted. I rushed off in search of a horse and buggy, two blocks further, and met a friend just getting into a buggy, to which was attached a dashing, fiery horse. I explained my desire, and in less than a moment Major Woodson and myself were driving furiously to the boat. No policeman interfered. The whistle had blown, steam up, and gang-ways ready to be hauled in, as we approached; we were just in time, the reins thrown over the horse's back, and into the boat we rushed, out of breath, but in time.

CHAPTER XIV.

WE START DOWN THE RIVER.

PRECISELY at the hour of 8 A. M. on the 22d of July, the Steamer "Farley" commanded by Captain Fry, pushed off from the landing at Columbus, ere we had time to look around. There stood our friend, Doctor Wyatt, tall, six-feet-one at least, thin and pale, his calm, quiet, and serene manner, calculated to inspire confidence and respect, but alas! not a believer in the code.

Doctor Courtney, with his gentlemanly and pleasant manners, greeted us cordially; and then, from out of the cabin, stepped our genial friend, Doctor King, his broad pleasant face not smiling, but with a mirthful glitter in the corner of his eye, which always rested there; his ample form seemed a boat-load in itself. He appeared perfectly at home; knew the captain, the mates, the cook, and everybody else, and was a code man every inch of him; now, however, engaged in the peaceable avocation of a Life Insurance Agent, taking this trip with us, as he said, merely for the purpose of insuring the lives of both parties, their seconds and friends. He said Miss ——— was the only lady passenger. He knew her, of course, and after awhile stepped into the after cabin to insure her life, but before doing so he had shown Major Woodson and myself to our state-rooms; pointed out to us the fact that the armory of the opposite party, consisting of several small swords, sabres, dueling pistols and guns, had been, by mistake, placed in our rooms. He requested our accommodating captain to have them removed, to keep from frightening us, he said. We now had leisure to enjoy the picturesque scenery as the boat quietly sped on its winding way down the beautiful Chattahoochee. At 10 A. M. we neared Abercrombie's Bend; there, upon the bank, stood Colonel Hercules D. Lofty, Captain Porter, and Major Shelton, but the boat passed on, and they were signalled to repair to a point some three hundred yards lower down, to be shipped.

At the point selected by Captain Fry as a safe place for his boat to touch the shore, the bank was precipitous, in fact nearly perpendicular; having been worn away for countless ages by the unceasing flow of the river at its base, it stood bare and naked, with an abrupt descent of nearly forty feet. The clay and sand which had, from time to time, fallen from the bank, formed a narrow bed at its foot comparatively level, and quite soft, and left an overhanging surface at the top, treacherous to look at, held there merely by the tenacity of the grass and shrub roots.

Winding down this cliff was a slippery footway, which we on the boat could see with tolerable distinctness, but was invisible to the party, now just discernible on the heights above.

We called aloud to them, and pointed out the place to enter this path. Finally, Captain Porter and Major Shelton saw our signs, and went towards it, but Colonel Lofty, marching onward with head erect, with that stately martial air which so becomes him, saw not our signals, heard not our voices raised to warn him of his danger, stepped out (with the boldness and decision so natural to him) upon the treacherous overhanging surface. Alas! what a fall was there—no, not a fall, but what a slide down the steep clay-stained cliff—clutching in desperation (as his false footing slid from beneath him) at shrubs and grass, as he slided on, even at the clay-bank itself, but all in vain! No power on earth could stop his slide until he rolled in the soft mud at the foot of the cliff, and there, while we stood spellbound upon the deck, we saw Colonel Lofty clutch desperately at his left thigh, and we feared some serious accident had befallen him. He rose slowly, still holding his thigh with both hands, and walked into the boat. He did not limp, but his erect carriage and dauntless air seemed for the moment to have deserted him.

He passed us by without a bow, right on into his state-room. His beautiful white vest was soiled, and his feelings, if not his limbs, evidently wounded.

Major Shelton and Captain Porter came quietly on board, both with pleasant manner and address.

The boat proceeded on its tortuous way. Doctor King walked around, knowing everything; the names of all the landings and bends, and where Miss ——— was to get off; when the boat would reach any given point; what we were to have for dinner—in short, everything worth knowing, with many an anecdote to beguile our way.

CHAPTER XV.

DOCTOR KING GIVES COMFORT AND OBTAINS A VALUABLE ACQUISITION.

At 12:20 P. M., Colonel Lofty emerged from his state-room, and before dinner was announced Doctor King was on terms of intimacy with him. Immediately after that important meal had been dispatched, Colonel Lofty requested Doctor King to do him the honor of granting a strictly private interview, and upon the request being acceded to, they repaired to a retired part of the boat, and had a serious and solemn conversation, which, as a true historian, I place before my readers, not so much because it bears directly upon the Code of Honor as because it is a fact. Their conversation was as follows:

Lofty. My dear Doctor King (bow), as I stood upon that steep and overhanging cliff, just before I did myself the honor of entering this boat, I observed you standing upon the after-deck.

King. Well, Colonel, I suppose you did. I certainly saw you.

Lofty. My dear Doctor King (bow), I observed at the same time that I had the pleasure of seeing you, a most beautiful lady standing by your side. Do you think now, my dear Doctor, that she saw me as I stood upon that high cliff or bank?

King. I don't see why she should not have seen you, for you were in plain view—in fact, the most conspicuous feature in the landscape.

Lofty. My dear Doctor, did you happen to notice that I entered the boat with—with—well, I may say, in some degree of haste—in short, that I walked down the bank somewhat rapidly—in fact, rather faster than I usually do myself the honor of walking?

King. Well, Colonel, if you call sliding down that bank, like a shot out of a shovel, except that you grabbed at everything in reach, "walking down the bank somewhat rapidly," I can tell you that I did happen to notice it.

Lofty. My dear Doctor, we will call it, then, my rapid approach to the boat, or we may say my—my—sliding down the bank. I have concluded to ask your opinion as to whether or not you thought that beautiful lady saw me—saw me—well, say, slide down that bank?

King. I think she did.

Lofty. My dear Doctor King (bow), did you happen to observe that immediately after the earth gave way, as I stood upon that high bluff, that I had the misfortune of having my pants come in contact with a snag, or root, situated near the top of the cliff, and, as I proceeded downward, that the snag still held my pants until a rent was made in them from just below the knee to the waistband?

King. Yes, Colonel, I saw it very plainly.

Lofty. My dear Doctor King, did you happen also to observe that, at the same time my pants were lacerated, my nether garment was torn in the same manner and by the same snag?

King. Of course, Colonel, I saw it all, for I was looking right at you.

"I Walked Down the Bank Somewhat Rapidly."

[*Page* 80.]

Lofty. My dear Doctor King, that beautiful lady standing by your side, do you think it possible that she saw—saw—anything?

King. Well, Colonel, I was really so interested looking at you slide down the bank that I did not turn to see whether "the beautiful lady," as you call her, had her eyes shut or not, but if you merely want my opinion, I rather think she kept them open.

Lofty. My dear Doctor (bow), I have some very fine whiskey in my state-room, and after the most remarkable and distressing events which have occurred in the last few hours, I feel that a drink is absolutely necessary to, in any degree, alleviate my feelings. I have already, since I had the honor of coming on this boat, taken several, but as there is still some on hand I hope you will do me the honor to join me (and they went inside).

As Doctor King described this scene to me, he attempted to imitate the courteous bow of Colonel Lofty, but I felt constrained to advise him that his effort was not quite successful. In the first place, I candidly expressed the opinion that no fleshy gentleman could ever accomplish it, for a respectable stomach made it a physical impossibility for the gentleman possessing it to descend more than one-third the distance requisite. Then the fingers of Doctor King's right hand were always more spread out when the one-third of the bow, which was all he could accomplish, was complete, than was allowable under the code. Of course I mentioned these points with the utmost delicacy, calling into play all the valuable lessons in politeness acquired during my intercourse with Colonel Lofty. So delicately did I express myself that Doctor King was perfectly satisfied with himself and with me, declaring, as we parted, that what perfection in bowing he should be able to acquire on the trip by constant practice, and association with Colonel Lofty, would be worth at least a thousand dollars to him in the Insurance business. He left me to renew an attempt to insure the life of one of the mates, who, he said, had resisted many a former effort. I noticed him approach the mate, bowing, with his idea of Colonel Lofty's urbane and courteous style. Half an hour later when we chanced to meet, his usually solemn face was radiant as he exclaimed, "Colonel, it worked like a charm. I have just insured that man's life for three thousand dollars. Had I understood bowing when among the Creek Indians the whole tribe would have taken policies."

I was pleased to see the contentment resting upon his countenance and said nothing to disturb it. He did not at all mind the scattering of furniture when in the way of performing his newly-acquired bow.

CHAPTER XVI.

AT EUFAULA.

At 3:18 P. M., our boat landed at Eufaula, a city noted far and wide for its beautiful women, and brave, chivalric men. As the boat was to remain here until 3 A. M., we went ashore, and found the city alive with rumors of the expected rencounter; dispatch after dispatch having been sent to this point and all other landings on the river blessed with a telegraph office, urging the arrest of both parties. The Governor of Florida had been telegraphed to have troops stationed at every landing in that State, and the Sheriff of Jackson County to have an armed posse at Neil's Landing, to prevent a fight at all hazards. Upon ascertaining these facts, Major Woodson and myself were on the point of re-embarking to avoid an arrest, when we had assurances from the courteous Mayor and resident officers, that no force, save that of moral suasion, would be used by them to prevent the bloody encounter expected in the sister State of Florida. Ministers of the Gospel and some old friends crowded around and implored me not to act rashly in the affair, but exhaust all honorable means for reconciliation. So much was I moved by their appeals that I assured them that neither Major Woodson nor myself desired a fight, and would only engage in one as a matter of accommodation. Doubtless I was wrong in making this frank admission. What would Colonel Lofty think, were he apprised of this confession? I attempted to repair my error by enjoining silence upon those who heard my expression, and my indiscretion would be forever buried, were it not that I consider it my duty, in this truthful history, to write it, because it is a fact.

Colonel Lofty was approached with the same solicitations, and while he received the parties making them with his usual courtesy, his greater experience and decision enabled him to impress it fully upon their minds that a meeting was inevitable. At 7:20 P. M., a self-constituted Board of Honor intervened without success.

At 9:32 P. M., Colonel Lofty was reported as having returned with his party to the boat. At 1:30 A. M., Major Woodson's friends were safely on board. At 2:08 A. M., Major Woodson and myself left the hotel for the boat and encountered an officer and posse, with a warrant for his arrest. Our position now seemed desperate. O, for the experience and coolness of Colonel Lofty in this emergency!

Should the arrest be made, there was absolutely no time to be released upon the States' most gracious writ of Habeas Corpus, that bulwark of liberty. I could think of nothing that Colonel Lofty would do if so situated, but invite the officer to drink—happy thought. My mind continuing to dwell upon that great man, it occurred to me that he would, at least, have bowed. Following the thought, I bowed profoundly, and when I recovered my upright posture, Major Woodson had disappeared in the darkness of the night.

After an ineffectual search, the officer returned to the spot where Major Woodson escaped, and I ascertained from him that the warrant he held had not been sued out by any citizen of Eufaula. A distant friend, who conscientiously believed that the code of honor was in conflict with the doctrines of the New Testament, had taken this means to prevent the shedding of blood. Now, under a strict construction of the code, this friend had no right thus to interfere, but as I have not consulted Colonel Lofty upon the point, do not lay it down as an absolute rule, and as the interference in this instance was ineffectual, I did not even advise Major Woodson to send a note to his officious friend.

CHAPTER XVII.

WHAT RUMOR SAID.

At the hour of 3 A. M., on the 23d day of July, our boat moved off from the Eufaula Landing. We were afloat again. Tired and sleepy we immediately repaired to the cabin, hoping to find an opportunity to enjoy the repose we so much needed; but there was a rumor aboard, which we were compelled to hear, in all its details, before we slept. This rumor was, as well as I can recollect, that Colonel Lofty had sat up with friends from the city until thirteen minutes after 2 A. M.; that these friends brought brandy with them, and that the Colonel had a large supply of whiskey on hand; that his friends drank whiskey with him and he brandy with them, until his equilibrium could no longer maintain its proper balance. Two boat-hands, said Madam Rumor, had been eye-witnesses to the fact that at the time, and in the state of mind and body above intimated, Colonel Lofty, with his friends, had approached the side of the boat, next to the bank, reeling to and fro like a tempest-driven ship in mid-ocean. She further reported that the Colonel, being prevented by one of the said boat-hands from completing the execution of a bacchanalian movement towards the edge of the boat, steadied himself for a moment, attempted to bow, and would have measured his length on the floor had it not been for the

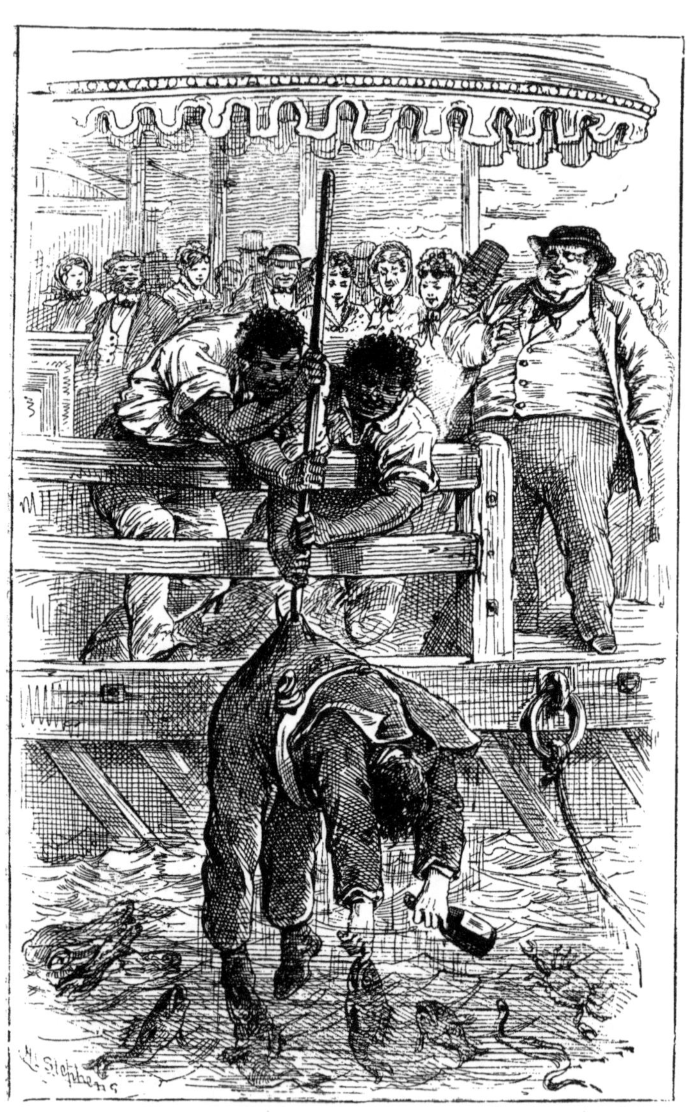

"And was Rescued from a Watery Grave." [*Page* 87.]

timely assistance of the other boat-hand. Feeling aggrieved at this imagined restraint upon his personal liberty, our author says that the Colonel gave vent to his indignation against the aforesaid boat-hands, threatening, in the vocabulary of the disciples of "John Barleycorn," to pull their noses or to send them a note "by a friend." And that, in this blissful state of mind, supported by a friend, he accidentally walked into the Chattahoochee, pulling his friend on top of him, and was rescued from a watery grave only by the prompt assistance of those on board.

Now all this is what rumor said, when we went aboard the boat, and it is narrated here because it is a fact that rumor said it. The tale that rumor told made a sad impression on my mind. It sorely grieved me to hear that Colonel Hercules Diogenes Lofty, my *beau ideal* of a great man, had become intoxicated and had fallen into the muddy Chattahoochee, and that, too, whilst engaged in conducting an affair of honor.

I retired to my berth a sad and disappointed man.

CHAPTER XVIII.

IT IS DEMONSTRATED THAT RUMOR CANNOT ALWAYS BE RELIED UPON.

WITH melancholy emotions did I dress myself and walk on deck, the morning following the occurrence of the events rumor related as having happened in the previous chapter. The first person it was my good fortune to meet was my friend Doctor Jones, who had joined us at Eufaula. He shook my hand, as usual, in a cordial manner, and inquired kindly after my health, remarking that I looked worse than he had ever seen me. I made a candid confession to him that I was suffering mentally, and informed him of all that rumor had said concerning the man with whose character I had been so favorably impressed. Listening to me patiently to the conclusion, his merry laugh resounded over the waters, and instantly reassured me in my favorable opinion of Colonel Lofty. "Colonel," said he, "that is all a mistake," and he thus explained the whole matter to my perfect satisfaction: "I was out early this morning, and met Colonel Lofty on the pass-way, back of his stateroom, watching for a waiter, and with nothing on but a shirt. In his left hand he held his pants, and over his left arm hung that beautiful white vest, which he wears so becomingly, and which you doubtless remember. In the Colonel's right hand was his coat, and suspended from his little finger were his boots, his arms being stretched out at full length to prevent any of the enumerated articles from coming in contact with his person, for they were soaking wet, and very muddy. With a bow, the Colonel responded to the salutation I addressed to him, expressing much happiness at seeing me, and requesting to know of me where I thought he could find a waiter so early in the morning.

"'I really cannot inform you, Colonel,' was my reply. 'We might call a boat-hand.' 'No! not a boat-hand,' said the Colonel, 'I would prefer not seeing one of them. You would oblige me by not calling one of them.'

"'Certainly not, Colonel, if you object,' I replied. 'I was distressed to hear this morning that an accident had befallen you—that you had fallen into the river.'

"'You do me great injustice, Doctor, unintentionally no doubt, by speaking of my having fallen into the river, or even of an accident having befallen me. I assure you, sir, there is a great mistake—an unpardonable error—existing in relation to the affair to which you have just alluded. Allow me to do myself the honor of explaining. Last evening my friend, Major Thorn, visited me socially and brought with him several gallons of the best whiskey I ever tasted, and about the same quantity of fine brandy. I am not very fond of brandy, when I can get whiskey, and I consequently confined myself, principally, to the whiskey. The evening passed off most pleasantly. Numerous friends dropped in upon us from time to time and honored us by drinking with us, and we continued to enjoy ourselves until eighteen minutes of two A. M., when, to my great surprise and mortification, I discovered that my friend, Major Thorn, was becoming intoxicated. Immediately upon making this discovery I insisted upon his going home. There is nothing that so mortifies me as to see a friend, even slightly inebriated, and I am always more particular on this point when an affair of honor is on hand. Prevailing upon my friend, by urgent entreaties, to leave me, we took a parting glass, and I accompanied him to the gangway, intending to see him off the boat in safety. (A boat-hand insulted me whilst I was in company with my friend, and I would have challenged him if he had been a gentleman.) The gangway of this boat consists of a plank just seventeen inches and a half wide. I pointed it out to my friend, as he was about to leave the boat, but being intoxicated, he insisted that it was not where I said it was, but just twenty-eight and a half inches to the right. A dispute ensued between us, and my friend, being intoxicated as aforesaid, concluded to split the difference, and in thus attempting to reach the shore walked into the river, missing the plank just fourteen and a quarter inches. Under such circumstances what was Hercules D. Lofty's duty? His guest had fallen into the river. He did what courtesy demanded, he immediately stepped into the water by the side of his friend, that his feelings might not be mortified by his being in the river alone. It was a mere act of courtesy to my guest, Doctor, that caused me to step into the river. No true gentleman could have done less under the circumstances.'"

I expressed to Doctor Jones my delight at hearing this reasonable, and doubtless correct version, of a circumstance that reflected so much credit on Colonel Lofty and so thoroughly exemplified his great delicacy of feeling.

"It was a mere Act of Courtesy to my Guest."

[*Page* 90.]

CHAPTER XIX.

INTERVIEWS BETWEEN DOCTOR KING AND COLONEL LOFTY.

WHILE Doctor Jones was giving me the satisfactory explanation detailed in the last chapter, Colonel Lofty quietly emerged from his state-room, fully dressed, except that his feet were only covered by a pair of socks, approached the state-room of Doctor King, who, fully dressed, was in the act of leaving it when he was accosted by Colonel Lofty as follows:

Lofty. My dear Doctor King (bow), may I be so bold as to inquire whether you have passed a pleasant night? I assure you that I feel pleased and much honored at seeing you.

King (attempting to bow). My dear Colonel, I slept well.

Lofty. My dear Doctor, I have done myself the honor of calling on you this morning in order that you might have the pleasure of conferring a great favor on me. I will remark, that last night I courteously stepped into the river after a friend, and in doing so had the misfortune of getting my boots damp, and this morning I found it impossible to place my feet in them, although I pulled off all the straps in making an attempt to do so. I have now temporarily parted with the possession of my boots, and placed them in the hands of the Steward of this boat, who is engaged in drying them. Now, my dear Doctor, I have had the honor of observing you wearing a pair of slippers, which (pardon me for noticing it) I now see on your feet (pointing to the large, flat-bottomed, low-quartered shoes on Doctor King's feet). Now, my dear Doctor, I wish to do myself the honor of borrowing those slippers from you; will you be so kind and obliging as to pull them off and let me wear them until my boots are dry (bow)?

King. My dear Colonel (attempting to bow), I assure you that it would give me pleasure to accommodate you in any way, but these "slippers" (as you call them) are the only shoes I have, and if I loaned them to you I would have to remain in my state-room barefoot, without the opportunity of insuring any one.

Lofty. My dear Doctor (bow), you astonish me beyond measure. I would have supposed that almost any gentleman would have provided himself with boots on such an occasion as the present. And now, as we are approaching the interesting spot where Captain Porter may send a note to Major Woodson, I would think that all the gentlemen in both parties would put them on. I assure you, sir, that never in all my great experience have I seen any gentleman approach a spot, selected as this has been, without boots.

King. My dear Colonel (attempting to bow), it may seem to you surprising, but it is not at all so to me. My business is a life-insurance agent, and I always succeed better in that business in flat-bottomed shoes. But allow me to say, that what surprises me beyond measure is, that a gentleman of your courteous manners, who is in the habit of stepping into rivers through courtesy to your friends, should not always provide yourself with slippers for such usual emergencies.

Lofty. My dear Doctor (bow), your remarks are correct and reflect credit upon yourself. Let me assure you that Hercules Diogenes Lofty always travels with slippers provided for just such emergencies as that of last night; but, sir, on this occasion, after my friend had fallen into the river and I had, through courtesy, stepped in and taken him out, I found that his boots were damp, and knowing that he would find a difficulty in getting them on this morning, I placed my slippers in his pocket that he might not be troubled in looking for his own when he should awake. Now, Doctor, I leave it to your honor whether a gentleman could do less under such circumstances?

King. My dear Colonel (attempted bow), I must say, that in my opinion you carry courtesy too far. I would think that courtesy could not have required more of you, under such circumstances, than to lend your friend one of your slippers, and then he could have hopped about until he found his own, and you could have done the same until you succeeded in borrowing one.

At 12 o'clock M. Doctor King was sitting on the deck of the boat when Colonel Lofty again approached, and, after a polite salutation, accompanied by the offer of a Havana cigar, addressed him as follows: "My dear Doctor King, there is on board this boat a trunk belonging to some member of Major Woodson's party, which is very heavy, as though it contained arms; now, my dear Doctor, would you be so kind as to honor me by surmising to which of Major Woodson's party that trunk belongs and what it contains?

King. Do you mean, Colonel, that large yellow trunk?

Lofty. My dear Doctor, that yellow trunk is the very

one to which I allude; it is an unusually long trunk, and looks as if it might contain shot-guns, unbreeched. Would you honor me, Doctor, by your views upon this subject?

King. Certainly, Colonel, I will take pleasure in doing so. I agree with you that the trunk might contain a shot-gun, unbreeched, and that it is heavy. I can also tell you what is in it, and to whom it belongs.

Lofty. My dear Doctor King (profound bow), you can have no idea how much pleasure you will confer on me by imparting this valuable information; confidentially, I will mention to you, my dear Doctor, that I have a great desire to know certainly whether Major Woodson has brought any arms. I would also be pleased to know what weapon he will select should a fight ensue, not that I would be influenced in the slightest degree by so immaterial a circumstance.

King. I propose to take one thing at a time. You ask first about the ownership of the yellow trunk and its contents. Well, that trunk belongs to me, and has my insurance papers in it. By the way, Colonel, could you not induce your friend, Captain Porter, to insure his life in one of the companies I represent?

Lofty. My dear Doctor King (bow), you must have quite a number of insurance papers; but I have not had the honor yet of hearing your views about the arms Major Woodson would select.

King. My dear Colonel Lofty, on that point I would advise you to consult Major Woodson, or his second; no doubt either would be glad to give you full information.

Lofty. My dear Doctor King (bow), you have no idea, sir, how distressed I feel on that very point. I have not the great honor and pleasure of knowing who Major

Woodson's second will be; now, my dear Doctor, I know that there are but few things of which you are not apprised, and I have seen you talking with Colonel Hurd and Major Woodson. Would you not be so kind as just to hint to me who will be Major Woodson's second, if you know?

King. Certainly I know.

Lofty. My dear Doctor, I felt confident that you knew. Will you please tell me at once?—not that it matters to me, for one man is the same as another in the eyes of Hercules Diogenes Lofty!

King. My dear Colonel (bow), in the first place, there is Colonel Hurd, then there is Doctor Jones, then Doctor Wyatt, then Doctor Grotius, and, finally, myself, all friendly to Major Woodson; and any of us, I presume, ready to act as his second, should necessity require it.

Lofty. Yes, my dear Doctor (bow), but *which* of these gentlemen is to be Major Woodson's second?

King. My dear Colonel, I will have to answer you, if you insist on it, as the showman answered the little boy.

Lofty. My dear Doctor (bow), I assure you, sir, that it would give me the greatest pleasure to hear how the showman answered the little boy, if you will be so kind as to inform me!

King. Certainly, Colonel; I have nothing else to do just now, and so I will tell you. There was once a showman who had nothing under his canvas but a small elephant and a large monkey. The price of admission was only twenty-five cents, and crowds came to see the show, each man and boy paying his quarter at the door. Well, sir, when the crowd had assembled, the showman very kindly explained to them, first, the habits and mode of life of the elephant; how that large animal, as a mere pastime, pulled up forest-trees by the roots, and fed himself with his snout, and drank rivers dry; together with many other interesting details about him. And then he explained all the habits of the monkey; telling about his activity; how he could jump forty feet up a tree, and twice as far down it; how he could climb a greased pole, and walk on his hind legs. Well, sir, after he was through, and the crowd were looking at the animals in silent admiration, a little boy stepped up and said: "I say, mister, will you please tell me which is y'r elephant and which is y'r monkey?" Then the showman answered the little boy, as I will have to answer you, Colonel.

Lofty. My dear Doctor, your story is very interesting, but *how* did the showman answer the boy?

King. Well, the showman looked at the little boy, and then said to him, "My friend, you paid twenty-five cents at the door to see these animals, and now look at them and take your choice." And, Colonel, if you have time, I will tell you another anecdote about a fox.

Lofty. My dear Doctor King, please excuse me, I would rather not hear another anecdote just at this moment. I am compelled to step back and see if my boots are dry.

And Colonel Lofty stepped into the cabin.

CHAPTER XX.

A DRINK OF CLARET, AND WHAT IT LED TO.

WHILE the last conversation, narrated in chapter nineteen, between Colonel Lofty and Doctor King, was progressing, I was invited by Major Shelton to join him in a glass of claret in the cabin. We were in the act of raising our glasses to our lips, after having clinked them together in the most approved dueling style, copying the example set by Colonel Lofty. This ceremony may, by the uninitiated, be thought useless, and I have heard it called vulgar by others. But nothing is more appropriate in affairs of honor. The sudden clink of the glasses mildly represents the pistol shots, and the drink following depicts the harmony and good feeling which is always the result of a meeting on the field of honor.

But I digress. At this moment Colonel Lofty entered; he started, stopped, and stood transfixed; his eyes, turned full upon me, seemed to pierce me through; then, gradually, he raised himself to such an erect position that his body was bent far backward, and he marched by me in stately grandeur; he did not speak, and his face seemed to denote rather grief than anger. I felt oppressed; and when Colonel Lofty returned to the outer air, made it a point to saunter near, and open a conversation with him, as follows:

Hurd. Colonel Lofty (profound bow), I hope that you experience no inconvenience from stepping into the river last night? I have had the honor to be informed that it was a mere act of courtesy, on your part, to a guest. Your noble action does you great honor, and reflects credit upon the gentlemen of this country, whom you so ably represent.

Lofty. Colonel Hurd (profound bow, and with a rather gratified expression in his eye), your remarks do me but justice, sir; and it reflects great honor on yourself that you are able to appreciate my act of courtesy. But, Colonel Hurd, you know I am a plain, blunt man. I hope you will pardon my mentioning the fact, that you, notwithstanding your uniform courtesy, have inflicted upon me a most severe and painful wound; you have deeply grieved me, sir, and caused me to suffer a pain such as no other man, except yourself, could inflict.

Hurd (with innocent and astonished air). My dear Colonel, how have I injured you?

Lofty. Colonel Hurd (bow), just fifteen minutes ago I did myself the honor of walking through the cabin; and, when there—ah! Colonel, your own heart tells you what I saw, and your own sense of honor tells you what I must have suffered. I did myself once the honor to explain to you the pain occasioned me by a similar act which I witnessed on the part of your friend Colonel Strong, but that was nothing compared with my feelings now; for, Colonel, I did you the honor to consider you one of the most courteous gentlemen I had ever had the pleasure of meeting, and, pardon me, you knew how I viewed your friend. Oh, Colonel, that you should have drank with Major Shelton, after having twice declined to drink with me, on the ground that you *never drank.*

Hurd. Colonel Lofty (bow), allow me to think that you do me a great injustice. I only drank wine with Major Shelton, at his polite invitation. How could I refuse him under the code, without doing myself and him dishonor, for I do sometimes drink wine? Had you asked me to drink wine, Colonel, I assure you that not for one moment would I have hesitated to drink with you. I hope you will do me the honor to recollect that you asked me to drink whiskey, and I refused, on the ground that I never drank whiskey.

Lofty. Ah, my dear Colonel (bow), while your excuse seems plausible, and relieves my feelings to some extent, yet I regret that you should, with me, deal in (pardon the expression) mere technicalities, a mere play upon words, sir, in a matter of so much importance, and where so much is at stake. You know, Colonel, how much honored I would have been by sending for a bottle of wine, so that I could have done myself the pleasure of drinking with you. Expense is nothing, sir, to Hercules D. Lofty, where honor is at stake. You must have guessed, Colonel, that I understood you to mean that you never drank at all.

Hurd. Colonel Lofty (profound bow), I submit it to your own delicate sense of honor, whether I could have acted otherwise than I did, under any principle of that high-toned courtesy so necessary in conducting an affair of honor. I was your guest. How could I, standing in that position, make a suggestion which might, by possibility, impose upon you either trouble or expense? I could not do it; but the point was so novel and interesting that I consulted not only the most noted duelists of my acquaintance, but all works on etiquette, and (pardon me for mentioning the fact) that my course was, by the great weight of authority, sustained. But I pause for your more experienced judgment.

Lofty. Colonel Hurd (bow), this is one of the most intricate and astounding points of etiquette that I have ever had the pleasure of encountering under the code; and, allow me to say, that you have raised yourself immensely in my estimation, by having had the honor of raising it. There can be no doubt, sir, that it reflects credit on your coolness, judgment, and keen sense of propriety, which I have rarely seen equalled. And, Colonel, I shall do myself the honor of agreeing with you, and I now propose that you will do me the honor of drinking with me generally. Select your own liquor, sir.

Hurd. Colonel Lofty (bow), it will afford me much pleasure to comply with your request.

And we drank, after having clinked our glasses together, and harmony was restored.

CHAPTER XXI.

NEIL'S LANDING.

At 12:42 P. M., on the 23d day of July, 1873, our boat reached Neil's Landing. The yellow trunk, and all our other baggage, consisting of divers articles necessary in adjusting affairs of honor, including the little brown jug, etc., were taken ashore.

No troops, police force, or sheriff, were present to interfere. And our agreeable landlord assured us, that under the law of Jackson County, Florida, every man, whether citizen or stranger, should do exactly as he pleased, and either drink or fight, as suited him best; that the practice with the citizens was, to drink first, which was necessary to keep off chills, and fight afterwards, to keep in practice.

We reached our comfortable lodgings, which had all the advantages of clean sheets, etc.; no guest having lodged in our hotel within the last eighteen months.

At 1:20 P. M., Colonel Lofty approached Major Woodson, and in the most artistic manner handed him the following note:

"NEIL'S LANDING, STATE OF FLORIDA,
"First floor of Hotel (name unknown).
"July 23d, 1873, 1 P. M.

"MAJOR JAS. F. WOODSON, *present en ville.*

"MY DEAR SIR:—You were kind enough to inform

me in Columbus, that you would receive a communication, which I had for you, at this place. I have the honor to inquire at what time it will suit your convenience, to receive that communication?

"I am, dear sir, respectfully,
"Your obedient servant,
"HERCULES D. LOFTY, M. D."

Major Woodson requested me to bear his reply to this polite note.

Finding Colonel Lofty in his apartments on the first floor of our hotel, the reply of Major Woodson was presented by me, and received by him, in a manner which did credit to both of us, and which was in accordance with the etiquette of the code in every particular, including drinks and bows. For Colonel Lofty, although he detested wine—in fact remarked, that it made him almost as sick as a drink of unmixed water—had a bottle expressly for my benefit.

Major Woodson's note, which was read during this interview, was as follows:

"NEIL'S LANDING, FLORIDA,
"July 23d, 1873, 1:25 P. M.

"COLONEL HERCULES D. LOFTY:

"SIR:—In reply to your note just handed me by yourself, I have the pleasure to state, that I will receive at any time, when it may suit your convenience, the communication which you have for me.

"I am, sir, respectfully,
"J. F. WOODSON."

At the hour of 3:15 P. M., Colonel Lofty, in his most urbane and stately manner, approached Major Woodson; each bowed low to the other, and then Colonel Lofty, first asking and obtaining permission, placed in Major Woodson's hands a note, which was in the following words and figures, "to wit:"

"NEIL'S LANDING, FLORIDA,
"July 23d, 1873, 3 P. M.

"MAJOR JAMES F. WOODSON:

"MY DEAR SIR:—In the Columbus 'Sun' of June 25th, over your signature, appears an advertisement which reflects most cruelly upon the memory of my deceased cousin. Whatever course the press may have seen cause to pursue, or anonymous writers may have chosen to publish, I submit was without either the knowledge or desire of his family, either immediate or remote. The allegations you make in that article are of an exceedingly painful character, and I am unwilling to believe that you would wantonly insult the memory of the dead, or gratuitously wound the feelings of the living. Therefore, I address you this letter, expressing the hope that you will disclaim all such intention, and request that you will withdraw every portion of that article, which reflects discreditably upon the memory of my deceased relative. This note will be handed you by my friend, Colonel H. D. Lofty.

"I am, sir, very respectfully,
"T. J. PORTER."

After reading this note, Major Woodson bowed low to Colonel Lofty, and Colonel Lofty bowed low to Major Woodson. And then Major Woodson informed Colonel Lofty that his reply would be presented by a friend. Then they both bowed and parted. Now, all was intense curiosity in the apartment where Major

Woodson's friends were assembled, to see the note which had been brought from the city of Atlanta, in the State of Georgia, to Neil's Landing, in Florida, to be delivered—that note which Colonel Lofty had so sacredly guarded; that note which Major Woodson had, from want of experience in these matters, presumed to be a hostile message; that note which the Major had in vain offered to receive in Columbus, Georgia. And upon its being exhibited, various were the remarks made. Meanwhile, I was lost in admiration at the remarkable foresight which had been evinced by Colonel Lofty. The prophets and soothsayers of ancient days could not be compared with him. Who but a man of such vast experience could have predicted, when that note was written in Atlanta, that the negotiations would finally result in Major Woodson selecting Neil's Landing? Who but Colonel Lofty could have foreseen that the boat would reach Neil's at the hour it did? Who but he would have had the delicacy of dating the note so as to fit these circumstances? And then I called to mind the pleasure Colonel Lofty had expressed to me at Major Woodson selecting that point. I could but express my admiration of all this foresight to my friends, when one of them, who had not seen the correspondence between Colonel Lofty and Major Woodson, remarked that he did not believe in predestination, and that he thought the note was written at the time and hour it bore date. But I convinced him of his error instantly, by exhibiting to him the former letters of Colonel Lofty, showing conclusively, that this note, which Major Woodson had come to Neil's Landing to receive, was in the possession of Colonel Lofty while in Columbus, and even the last note signed by that gentleman tended to prove the same fact. Major Woodson concluding to take time to answer this polite note, inasmuch as it only asked for a withdrawal of certain statements, and not for a meeting, we dispersed, and I had a casual conversation at 3:30 P. M., with Colonel Lofty, in which I intimated this fact to him ; but as that conversation is set out pretty fully at Colonel Lofty's request, in a letter which I did myself the honor of writing to him, I omit to give it here, referring the curious reader to the letter itself, which is copied in chapter XXXV., in this volume.

CHAPTER XXII.

AS TO WHETHER AN INTERMEDIATE NOTE SHOULD BE DELIVERED.

After the occurrence of the events narrated in chapter twenty-first, Major Woodson and myself strolled about the country until nearly dark. Upon our return we were met by the urbane Colonel Lofty, who requested a private conference with me, which I politely acceded to, and we discoursed as follows:

Lofty. Colonel Hurd (bow), have you a note from Major Woodson to Captain Porter, requesting to be allowed time to answer?

Hurd (bow). Certainly not, Colonel Lofty. Major Woodson does not expect to do himself the honor of writing such a note.

Lofty. Colonel (bow), you surprise me beyond measure. I certainly understood you to say, in our informal conference, that Major Woodson would do himself the honor of writing such a note.

Hurd. Colonel Lofty (bow), I hope you will permit me to say, respectfully, that you misunderstood me. I assure you that no such thought ever entered my mind, for Major Woodson had concluded to write nothing until he formally answered Captain Porter's note. In the first place, he thinks this is the proper course under the code, and in this view I concur with him. In the next place the *friend* of his choice is not with him.

Lofty. Colonel Hurd, I am compelled to pain myself by differing with you on your first point, and allow me to say, Colonel, that you should yield to my greater experience in these affairs. I assure you, sir, that I am always correct—a written note must have a written answer.

In nineteen of the affairs of honor which I have had the honor to conduct, this point was raised under Wilson's Code, and in each of them I required an intermediate answer, respectfully asking time to reply. I never had any serious contest over this point but once, when I felt myself compelled to challenge the opposing second, whose opinion differed from mine, which delayed the original affair eight hours and twenty-three minutes, as I had the pain of killing my antagonist at the first shot. I always fire before the word "one," and almost invariably hit my antagonist just above the right eye. In the particular case to which I refer, the new second, selected on the demise of the first, immediately agreed with me in my construction of the code.

Hurd. While my respect for your judgment in such matters, Colonel, is almost unlimited, yet in this instance, as my opinion differs from yours, I am impelled reluctantly to decline the honor of having you manage both sides of this interesting affair. The code, if I am not in error, does not require an instantaneous answer.

Lofty. Colonel Hurd (bow), let me beseech you as a friend to reconsider. I assure you I have only Major Woodson's honor in view in offering you this advice. Allow me to have the pleasure of saving his honor. I am satisfied that you can no longer refuse my request when I inform you, that so well do I know my position to be correct, that I shall, if you do not accede to it, remain at this place with my principal for the next forty-six days. I know, Colonel, that you would not inflict this punishment upon me. The mosquitoes are terrible, and there are no "bars," and our landlord says, that no man can remain here more than a week without having fever and ague; then the whiskey, I assure you, Colonel, is not fit to drink. I had almost as soon drink wine, or even water. Oh, Colonel, it will be terrible, but my honor will compel me to stay, and Hercules D. Lofty will do what honor demands.

Hurd. Colonel Lofty (bow), while I deeply regret your decision upon your own account—for the mosquitoes I know to be bad, and from your description the whiskey is equally so—yet, being convinced that Major Woodson is right in his decision, I can not advise him, even after knowing your views differ from mine, to alter his opinion. We leave here at 8 P. M., on the next boat, and if you adhere to your determination to remain, I will do all in my power to alleviate your suffering. I can ship your mosquito bars and a barrel of whiskey by next boat from Eufaula, and any other commission I will be only too happy to execute.

Lofty. Colonel Hurd, I beg you to consider the expense, and the suffering I must endure, before the bars and whiskey, you so kindly offer to ship, can reach me; and if you are not willing to trust my judgment upon this point, I hope you will be willing to leave it to the decision of Captain Porter's Surgeon, Doctor Courtney.

Hurd. Colonel Lofty (bow), if you will do me the honor of returning with us on the next boat, I will agree that Doctor Courtney and General Rock may consider this point when we arrive at Columbus, and should they decide that an intermediate note is necessary or proper, it shall there be written and ante-dated as if sent from this point.

Lofty. Colonel Hurd (bow), I will, with your permission, take twelve minutes to consider your proposition, after the termination of this most interesting conversation; and, Colonel, allow me now to remark, that I know Major Woodson came here prepared to fight, and brought arms with him.

Hurd. Ah, Colonel! will you do me the honor of mentioning who informed you that Major Woodson had arms with him?

Lofty. My dear Colonel (bow), I have no accurate information on the subject, but I am willing to leave it to you on your honor to say, whether he has arms with him, for I know you are the soul of honor and would scorn to be untruthful in anything.

Hurd. Colonel Lofty (bow), if you leave it to my honor I will be compelled to honor you and myself by answering, that if Major Woodson has arms with him, he has certainly made no display of them. Allow me to hope, Colonel, that this answer gives all the information you desire.

Lofty. Certainly, Colonel, I was not seeking information.

And we bowed and parted, and in twelve minutes afterwards the proposition of arbitrament was accepted, and we were all rendered happy by the prospect of Colonel Lofty's company on our return.

Just before the boat arrived, our loquacious landlord (whom I take pleasure in recommending to all duelists in the country) approached me mysteriously and said, with a very fair dueling bow, "Colonel, as I told you the law of Jackson County is all right on fighting, but, sir, there is a newspaper published in this county, which is always meddling in other people's concerns, and I just know they will send a man up here to pump me about this matter; now, what tale must I tell him?" I said, "My friend, tell him the truth. Let that paper print the truth once, as an example to all other papers." "But, Colonel," said he, "I don't know the truth about this matter." I replied, "Well, my friend, just tell the truth, as far as you know it. No man knows the whole truth, but let every man tell it as far as he knows." "Well, then, Colonel, I will tell the newspaper man that neither party came here to fight, but that you and Colonel Lofty are the two politest men I ever saw."

At nineteen minutes past 8 P. M., the up-river boat left Neil's, with both parties on board, homeward bound. At eleven minutes after 9 P. M., the Woodson party had retired to their state-rooms.

CHAPTER XXIII.

DOCTOR KING SEARCHES FOR A DRINK.

At 5:06 A. M. Doctor King awoke, with a sensation in his throat as if he had been swallowing dry cotton, and some of it had lodged therein.

At this early hour no ladies were astir, and hence Doctor King emerged from his state-room in his night-dress—consisting only of a shirt, which, not being confined in his pantaloons, as usual with him in the day, hung out from his body very much like a lady's dress, except that it was not half so long—made his way through the boat, and awoke Major Woodson and his friends, in his search for a drink; and, after they had been thus aroused, several of them complained of having a sensation in their throats as if they had been swallowing dry cotton, and some of it had lodged; but on examination it was found that none of them had any spiritous, vinous, or malt liquors—their supply had been exhausted.

Then Doctor King, in his night-dress aforesaid, awoke the captain, mates, stewards, and cook of the boat, for the same object, and with a like unpleasant result. The Doctor, now being desperate, and the sensation of dry cotton in his throat becoming more and more annoying, seized a tumbler in his right hand, approached Colonel Lofty's state-room, touched the Colonel, and then actually shook him; finally Colonel Lofty "did himself the honor to awake," and looking out of his berth perceived the bowing figure of Doctor King, apparreled as last aforesaid. The courteous Colonel cast his eyes upon the glass in Doctor King's hands, but delayed making any remark until he had raised himself in his berth to a sitting posture; then he said, "My dear Doctor King (bow as profound as the limits of his berth would admit), I will, with pleasure, sir, do myself the honor of drinking with you; and allow me to remark, that it is most kind and courteous in you, my dear Doctor, to come around and bring me a drink, at this early hour of the morning. In fact, sir, it is a courtesy I have rarely seen equalled under the code;" and he held out his hand for the glass in the Doctor's hand. Doctor King bowed and said, "My dear Colonel, excuse me, I have just called on you for the purpose of getting a drink, as none of Major Woodson's party have a drop. This glass is empty, and I have failed to find any on the boat. Will you be so kind as to allow me to have access to your 'little brown jug?'"

Colonel Lofty exclaimed, "Oh! my dear Doctor, how you have disappointed me! My friend, Doctor Courtney, and myself, sat up last night and drank all we had left. Oh! oh! (placing his hands on his person, just below his breast) I would give one hundred dollars for a drink of whiskey."

"It is a Courtesy I have rarely seen equaled under the Code."

[Page 112.]

CHAPTER XXIV.

COLONEL LOFTY'S OPINION OF THE PRESS.

At 9 A. M. of the 24th of July we touched at Fort Gaines, and shipped a small quantity of whiskey. At 12 M. we arrived at Eufaula, and here the boat stopped long enough to take in a full supply of liquors, and here we found the morning papers from Columbus, Georgia. At 12 : 50 P. M., just thirteen minutes after we left Eufaula, all of us were standing on deck, smoking, when Colonel Lofty approached me—not in his usual manner, but with indignation depicted on his countenance—a newspaper in his hand.

"Colonel Hurd," said he (omitting his bow), "have you seen this infamous and insulting piece in the 'Sun?'" "I have not, as yet, done myself the honor to read the 'Sun,'" I replied.

"Then," said Colonel Lofty, "I will inflict upon myself the pain of reading this horrible piece to you, sir ; but first allow me to make a remark : I hold, that a gentleman's name belongs to himself, and that no man has a right to use it, write it, or print it, without having first obtained permission from the owner. Gentlemen do not want notoriety—we wish to live in a quiet and retired manner, apart from shop-keepers, policemen, and mere men of business ; in a quiet manner, sir, that permits us to settle our affairs of honor in our own way.

What gentleman wants his name advertised and vended about in an infamous sheet, like the inventor of some quack medicine? It cannot be submitted to, Colonel! Hercules D. Lofty and George W. Hurd will let the world know, that their names are never to be used, unless permission is first obtained. Just hear me read the false and lying remarks of this filthy little sheet:—

"'The Reported Duel:—For a number of days the streets have been full of rumors of a duel between Major James F. Woodson, of Alabama, and Mr. Porter, of Atlanta, Georgia. The quarrel is said to have originated from an advertisement, published in this paper, commenting upon the evidence offered in a lawsuit, so far as it related to the personal character of a Mr. Thomas K. Smith, deceased. The Major was one of the counsel. Report states that Mr. Porter demanded a retraction, which Major Woodson refused. Yesterday, Major W. left here on the steamer "Farley." Colonel Lofty, who is acting for Mr. Porter, with his principal, and a Major Shelton, left the city early yesterday morning, intending to take the boat at Woolfork's. Among those who took the boat here were Colonel G. W. Hurd—said to be Major Woodson's second—and Doctors King, Jones, and Wyatt. All matters connected with the affair are kept very close, but the general report is, that a challenge will be passed at Neil's Landing, in Florida. Mr. Porter has not registered at any of the hotels, and we do not know his given name. We hope the affair can be settled without a fight; rumors are plentiful, and almost worthless. A telegram received states that the boat passed Eufaula last night, and no arrest made.'"

After reading this article, Colonel Lofty proceeded: "Now, Colonel Hurd, you will at once perceive that every word in this piece is a most wilful falsehood." Doctor Wyatt said, in a mild, conciliatory manner, "I do not look on it exactly in that light, Colonel; there may be some errors, but I suppose they were unintentional." Colonel Lofty proceeded, "Colonel Hurd, you, sir, being a lawyer, know the force of the maxim, '*Falsus in uno, falsus in omnibus*,'" and turning to the others, who were supposed not to be so learned, he said, in English, "'To be false in one thing, proves that a man is false in all.' It is a maxim handed down to us from the time that the Roman Empire was in its pristine glory, and has always proved true; it is now even entered upon our law-books—as Colonel Hurd will testify. Now, look at this malicious piece; do you not see it states that I, Hercules D. Lofty, intended to take the boat at Woolfork's, when, in fact, I did myself the honor of stepping on the boat, on the opposite side of the river, at Abercrombie's Bend?" "I would amend by saying, slided down to the boat," suggested Doctor King. Colonel Lofty turned to the speaker with an indignant air, but, before answering the untimely suggestion, his kindness of heart intervened, and he only said, "Oh, Doctor, please consider that this is no time for a joke, or a play upon words. The honor of all of us is at stake, and Hercules D. Lofty will protect it. We all know the statement I have referred to is false; it therefore follows, that every word and letter of this infamous and scurrilous squib is false. If I am not correct in this assertion, then the maxim is false—which is impossible. Now, Hercules D. Lofty places a higher value upon truth than upon any other thing in this world, or the next; for truth is honor, and honor is truth, and, for a man to be untruthful, or to prevaricate even in the smallest particular, fills me with untold horror. A man who is untruthful is worse than an infidel. Now I have concluded to challenge the local editor of this paper, and, Colonel Hurd, I have done myself the honor to select you as my second, to bear my note to this man." I replied, "Colonel Lofty, you do me great honor, but inasmuch as I am so situated as to make it impossible for me to act, either as principal or second, in an affair of honor at this time (as I have heretofore explained to you), I hope you will do me the kindness to excuse me. Were I differently situated, nothing would give me more pleasure than to act for you." Colonel Lofty said, smiling and bowing, "Colonel, I know that you are so situated as to be unable to act, and I therefore excuse you; but, sir, I demand of you, that you appoint one of your party to bear my message. I think it proper that this matter should be represented by both parties. I will do the fighting, and I only require a second from your party."

I replied, "Colonel, I will readily comply with your reasonable request; allow me first to appoint them all, Doctor Wyatt, Doctor King, Doctor Jones, Doctor Grotius; please approach them, Colonel, and ascertain which of them is most anxious to act for you, in this important affair, and inform that gentleman from me, that I give my full consent to his acting—as he pleases."

Colonel Lofty thanked me kindly, and in turn approached each of the gentlemen named, but each being convinced that nothing but blood could alleviate his outraged feelings, declined to act for him, all of them being friends of Captain De Soto, the editor in question. So well was I acquainted with the high-toned, sensitive nature of Colonel Lofty, that I expected him to challenge each one of the gentlemen refusing, and he would undoubtedly have done so, but a happy idea changed the current of his thoughts; he called both of our parties together and invited us to drink; we drank—then adjourned to the lower deck, and sat around on some empty coffins, shipped at Eufaula; then Colonel Lofty arose from his seat on the largest coffin and remarked, "This piece, which I hold in my hand, is a most infamous one; and, on reflection, I must think that the man who wrote it is devoid of truth, and therefore not entitled to be noticed by me—for no man can be a gentleman who is not truthful in every particular. It has occurred to my mind to mention how I once acted in a similar case. One of the first editors in one of our largest cities, had caused my name to be printed in his paper, without first asking permission, and had the impudence to make some remarks about me, which I considered insulting, though not to be compared with this scurrilous piece. I purchased a large cowhide, walked quietly into his sanctum, where I found him with his coat off; without saying a word I took him by the collar and gave him four cuts across his face, and three over his left shoulder. I then notified him that a full and ample apology must be printed in his paper next day, or I would use my cowhide freely upon his person. Next day a most handsome apology was published. That editor now, before printing my name, invariably sends round a polite note, asking permission to do so, with a copy of the piece he proposes to print. Now, I am inclined to take a similar course in this most remarkable case." Doctor Wyatt said he thought a more temperate method might be adopted, and be equally beneficial to all parties, but Colonel Lofty's indignation, having been aroused by the falsity of every word in the article alluded to (which he had so unanswerably demonstrated), remained obdurate, and announced that the conference was ended, and that "the little brown jug" awaited us in his state-room. Upon repairing to the point indicated, we found the statement of this remarkable man to be true in every particular, more true than his modesty had allowed him to state, for not only was the jug there, but "the scent of the whiskey remained round it still," and a flask of wine set aside for Major Shelton and myself, whom Colonel Lofty facetiously called, "the light brigade."

CHAPTER XXV.

MORE ABOUT THE SLIDE.

DURING the afternoon of the 24th of July, Colonel Lofty approached me, and remarked: "Colonel, you doubtless heard the expression used by our dear friend, Doctor King, about my *sliding* down to the boat. Now I am opposed to jokes, and our friend, Doctor King, does nothing, that I can see, but tell anecdotes about monkeys and other animals, and crack jokes; and, permit me to say, that I consider some of his jocular remarks, as (pardon me) neither witty nor appropriate, on such an occasion as this, or during the pendency of any affair of honor. Now the remark to which I refer, jarred very much upon my sense of honor and propriety. The point I was proceeding to discuss, at the time of his interruption, was one in which his honor was almost as deeply involved as my own, and his jocular way of saying, that I, Hercules D. Lofty, *slided* into the boat, was very painful to me. Is Hercules Diogenes Lofty, M. D., a piece of timber, to be *slided* about?"

Hurd. It is rather a difficult problem, Colonel, to find an expression which conveys the exact truth, and at the same time is compatible with your dignity, which must be upheld at all hazards; but allow me to suggest the words: your "*dashing descent,*" in lieu of your "*slide,*" as Doctor King terms it.

Lofty. Colonel Hurd (bow), permit me to thank you for the suggestion you have so kindly made, and while I really see no necessity for alluding to the circumstance at all, yet, if it should be alluded to in future, I would greatly prefer that the expression you suggest should be adopted. Will you do me the favor, Colonel, to inform your friends that I prefer it? I have no doubt, Colonel, that you saw and appreciated the cause of my—of my "dashing descent."

Hurd. Certainly; the overhanging bank gave way, and you, unintentionally, came down with it. Such accidents sometimes occur, even where every precaution has been taken to avoid them.

Lofty. Ah! Colonel, you do me great injustice. I would have thought that your great power of observation might have enabled you to see the occurrence in its true light. Allow me to explain it; but before doing so, permit me to remark, that it was not an accident, sir. I am not a creature of accident! No, sir; Hercules D. Lofty never allows himself to be swerved from his course by accident. And neither was my—my "dashing descent" unintentional. No, Colonel. I had under my care and protection, the lives and honor of my friends. I saw at a glance, the extreme danger of the position; my friends were approaching a precipice, where a false step might result in death. What was my duty under such circumstances? Hercules D. Lofty did his duty; he stepped boldly forward, taking all the danger upon himself. I well knew, I admit, that my remarkable presence of mind, and coolness in the most imminent peril, would, in all probability, save my life, where the want of those admirable qualities in my friends might have proved their destruction. My effort to save them was successful. By my bold and prompt action, I demonstrated to my friends where the dangerous part of the precipice was, and they were enabled to come down by a safe route, and my own wonderful presence of mind prevented any injurious results to myself. I suppose you noticed, Colonel, when that snag had inserted itself into and through my pants and drawers, the great coolness I displayed in turning my body slightly, so as to effectually prevent its being stuck through my thigh? Now I hope, my dear Colonel, that you will explain this matter, so that no report may be started, discreditable to my judgment, about an accidental fall.

Hurd. Your noble action does you infinite credit, and should be recorded in history. It will afford me pleasure to see that this incident is viewed in its true light.

At this moment Doctor King approached, eating the back-bone of a chicken, which the cook had kindly reserved for him, and remarked, "I am sorry we pass 'Abercrombie's Bend' in the night. I wanted to get another look at that place. In case any one should inquire about it when we get home, I would like to be able to give an accurate description of it. By the way, gentlemen, that calls to mind a most interesting anecdote, and as we have nothing else to do, I will relate it. There was a man who——

Lofty. My dear Doctor, pardon me for interrupting you; but you will find these Havanas very fine. Will you honor me by trying one? (offering them to both of us).

King. My dear Colonel, I am much obliged (taking a cigar, and putting it in his pocket). You will pardon my putting this cigar in my pocket. I am not quite through with my snack, and, besides, you know I can never tell an anecdote while I am smoking; and as you seem so much interested in the one I have just commenced, I will not deprive you of the benefit of it by lighting my cigar. Well, there was a man who had a most remarkable dog—that dog——

Lofty. Pardon me, my dear Doctor, for again interrupting you; but I have some important letters to write, and hope you will excuse me (and he bowed, and retired).

Doctor King's face was radiant, his eyes twinkling, and his sides shaking with laughter (probably at the recollection of the incidents in his proposed anecdote), but he refused to proceed with his recital of it to me, saying, that he would wait until Colonel Lofty was at leisure to hear it. "He cannot possibly stay in that cabin more than ten minutes, for I have just come through it, and it is hot enough in there to barbecue a hog. It is perfectly suffocating, without a particle of fresh air. I tell you, Colonel, he can't stand it. He will have to come out in a very few minutes, to get air." And again the fat sides of the Doctor shook with suppressed laughter, until it seemed to impart a trembling motion to the boat.

But Doctor King was mistaken in supposing that Colonel Lofty would abandon the cabin, before his self-imposed task was completed. It is true, that several times the Colonel came to the door and looked out during that sweltering afternoon; but on Doctor King's calling to him to come out, and stating that he had reserved his seat near us, in the most pleasant part of the boat, Colonel Lofty politely declined the invitation, on the ground that he had not completed his letters, and re-entered the cabin. Each time this was repeated, the trembling motion was imparted to the boat, by the shaking of Doctor King's sides.

It pained me to think, that the duty of writing those important letters should have confined Colonel Lofty to the uncomfortable cabin for so long a time.

CHAPTER XXVI.

THE INTERMEDIATE NOTE QUESTION.

As the sun rose, on the morning of the 25th of July, we arrived in Columbus, and General Rock was immediately notified that he and Doctor Courtney had been selected to decide the momentous question as to whether, under Wilson's Code, it was necessary that Major Woodson should write a note to Captain Porter, politely requesting the latter to allow a specified period of time, in which to answer his note of 23d of July.

At 10 A. M. these gentlemen proceeded to investigate this important subject. After a prolonged and patient investigation no precedent could be found, embracing the precise point, which sustained Major Woodson's view.

Upon the other hand were the nineteen precedents, embracing this precise point, recollected by Colonel Lofty, but which had never been published, owing to the remarkable modesty of that great man, and to which there remained no living witness except himself. Each one of these precedents fully sustained Colonel Lofty's proposition. One of them being of so high a character as to have cost a gentleman holding an opposite opinion his life. So far, then, as regarded precedents, Colonel Lofty's position seemed impregnable.

And Doctor Courtney, upon an examination of the entire subject, was of opinion that it was correct.

General Rock, however, appearing to disregard the nineteen precedents, and applying himself to the high reason of the code, was of opinion, that only one reply was necessary, and that it might be made at any period within the time allowed by the code. And in the present instance, that an intermediate reply was unnecessary.

At 9 P. M. the question remained undecided. At 9:45 P. M. an umpire was called in, who decided that a short note, stating that an answer would be made in the usual time, would not be inappropriate, and, inasmuch as it was desired by Colonel Lofty, it might be considered courteous to send it informally. Thereupon the following note was written, and, by one of the arbitrators, handed to Colonel Lofty:

"NEIL'S LANDING, July 23d, 1873.

"SIR:—I have received your note of this date, and will reply within the usual time.

"I have the honor to be, respectfully,

"J. F. WOODSON.

"To Captain T. J. PORTER."

Whether the umpire weighed fully the nineteen precedents I am unable to inform my readers. And it is to be regretted that the question is still an open one. Standing thus, eighteen simple and one fatal precedents, remembered by Colonel Lofty, in favor of the necessity of sending an intermediate note, asking to be allowed time, against one simple precedent, an arbitration with a divided board in favor of the propriety of an intermediate note announcing that an answer would be made within the usual time.

While this arbitration was in progress, Colonel Lofty,

after courteously drinking with each friend, whom he did himself the honor to meet, repaired to the "Sun" office and there met Captain De Soto.

What occurred during that important interview I regret to say cannot be narrated with the accuracy and precision so desirable in this history; and inasmuch as the recollection of Colonel Lofty upon the subject is stated in a letter to myself, dated 23d August, 1873, copied in chapter XXXII.; and, as the recollection of Captain De Soto, being diametrically opposed to that of Colonel Lofty, is stated in the clippings from the press herein contained, my own recollection of their interview is intentionally omitted. The fact that I was not present thereat induces me the more readily to adopt this course.

CHAPTER XXVII.

AT OPELIKA.

On the morning of the 26th of July the following article appeared in the "Sun:"

"From personal information received from Colonel Hercules D. Lofty, we state that the article published in yesterday's 'Sun' was erroneous in many particulars. We therefore withdraw the article in toto, regretting that we have, on the strength of rumors and telegrams, connected the names of Colonel Hercules Diogenes Lofty, M. D., Major Shelton, and Captain Porter, in so mortifying a position."

On the same day I repaired to Opelika, and, upon stepping from the cars on my arrival, had the honor of meeting Colonel Lofty, Major Shelton, and Captain Porter, and was informed that we had traveled on the same train, but in different coaches. What my readers and myself have lost by my failure to travel in the same coach with Colonel Lofty, and hear his varied conversation, can never be known, for the Colonel never repeats, except on bows and drinks.

Immediately on my discovery of Colonel Lofty and his party, I approached and requested them to do me the honor of walking over to Dunbar's sample rooms, for the purpose of taking a parting drink

To my astonishment, Colonel Lofty politely declined my invitation; his refusal was so unexpected that I could, at the moment, make no reply, when the Colonel, with that penetration which is one of his distinguishing traits, observing my embarrassment, remarked, "Colonel, I assure you that it is from no feeling of disrespect that I decline your most courteous offer, but I have on hand an affair of such vast importance to my personal honor as to make my acceptance impossible at this moment; and it is but courteous that I should state the nature of the business which now engages my attention, as an excuse for declining to drink with you. When you hear me, I am satisfied that you will do me the justice to say that I am right in even going so far as to postpone a drink, to accomplish my object. This train remains here only half an hour; I intend pursuing my journey to Atlanta upon it.

"You are aware of how grossly I was insulted in Columbus, by Colonel Strong. Well, sir, I have put myself to the trouble of preparing a most humble apology, for Colonel Strong to sign, which states, among other things, that he considers himself a low dog, and begs me to forgive him for the wrong he has done me, and promises to make a similar apology in the next issue of his paper. I propose to make him sign this paper instantly. If you, Colonel, will be so kind as to show me his office, I will probably be through with this little affair in less than five minutes, for I do not intend to allow Colonel Strong to speak, but merely let him sign this paper. I do not think I shall even take the trouble to read it to him. When it is signed, Colonel, if there is time, I will do myself and you the honor of drinking with you."

I bowed low and said, "Colonel, I think it will probably be longer than you at present calculate before Colonel Strong's signature is affixed to that paper, although it reflects credit on yourself that you should be willing even to postpone a drink, not to speak of the danger of your present undertaking, to save your honor."

Colonel Lofty straightened himself to his most erect position and looked me in the eye. I saw at once that some portion of my remark had "grieved" him. He said, "Will you please explain what you mean by your remark, Colonel Hurd, 'That it will be longer than I calculate before I compel Colonel Strong to sign this paper?' I said five minutes, sir, and Hercules D. Lofty never lies. Colonel, please pardon my insisting on an explanation from you."

I replied, with my most polite bow, "Colonel, you are aware that Colonel Strong left this point, for North Carolina, about the time we left Columbus for Neil's Landing, and it is reasonable to suppose that his return by this time is a most improbable event."

Colonel Lofty said, with his usual courteous salutation, "Colonel Hurd, it does me honor to accept your excuse, and as you think Colonel Strong has not returned, I will now do myself the pleasure of drinking with you, at the place which you were so kind as to indicate."

And we walked over to the bar-room. As we went Colonel Lofty requested me to inform Colonel Strong, on his return, that he had called to see him, but to say nothing as to the object of his visit, for, he said, "Although Colonel Strong has injured me so deeply, I do not desire to make his degradation more public than may be necessary to sustain my own honor." Mark the magnanimity of the man!

After we had imbibed of the best at Dunbar's, Colonel Lofty did me the honor to take me aside and remark, "Colonel, I have been considering this affair between Captain Porter and Major Woodson, and have come to the conclusion that it may possibly be settled without bloodshed. I feel a great interest, not only in preserving the life, but also the honor of Major Woodson. I assure you, Colonel, that I have nothing in the world against Major Woodson, except one remark, which he made on our trip. I had asked him most courteously to do me the honor of drinking with me, and he replied, that he had just taken a drink, and preferred keeping his nerves steady, to drinking any more; now, I might have excused him under the circumstances had he not added, 'But, Colonel, as it is you who do me the honor to offer the drink, I will take a little, just to show you that I do not think the liquor you offer me is *poisoned*.' I drank first to show Major Woodson that he was mistaken in supposing that Hercules D. Lofty would poison liquor. I could not resent the insult at the time, because the original affair was pending, but I propose to send him a note, as soon as we can arrange the matter between himself and Captain Porter; and, as I had the honor of remarking to you, I have now come to the conclusion no blood need necessarily be spilt in that affair. The mode in which I propose to settle it is, that Major Woodson write just a short note to Captain Porter, which I will do myself the honor to dictate, stating in substance that he deeply regrets his error, and hopes that Captain Porter will forgive him. In this simple manner the lives and honor of both parties can be saved. I think such a note will be satisfactory to Captain Porter."

I bowed and said, "Colonel, I have no doubt that your suggestion is prompted by that kindness of heart which does you so much honor, yet in this instance it is useless. You are aware that I am not, and will not be, Major Woodson's second; when his second is selected, Major Woodson's honor will be in his hands. It would, you know, Colonel, be indelicate in me to offer any advice to either. Could I overcome these scruples, I could not, Colonel, consent to assist in placing you in so false an attitude as you would occupy should it appear that you attempted the conduct of both sides of this most intricate affair. I doubt not that you would fill the delicate position with more than ordinary prudence, but you know it is so usual to have each side represented by different parties. Colonel, would you honor me by your views on this point?"

Colonel Lofty said, that the information he had given me about the note which, in his opinion, should be written, was strictly confidential, and that he wished me on no account ever to mention it. "In fact I would prefer that it should never be known, that Hercules D. Lofty, even in the strictest confidence, intimated the character of the note which Major Woodson should write in reply to that of Captain Porter."

Of course, Colonel Lofty was assured by me that the suggestion he had so kindly made would never be referred to. And of course it never was referred to. And, hence, no benefit was derived therefrom in this affair. It is only recorded here because it is a fact, and may be useful in some future duel.

After this conversation we lighted our cigars, and bowed and parted.

CHAPTER XXVIII.

COLONEL LOFTY'S CARD.

On the twenty-eighth of July, 1873, I had the pleasure of receiving through the mail, a copy of the "Herald" from Colonel Lofty, containing a card from himself; and as this card refers to Wilson's Code, and, at the same time, lays down rules greatly in advance thereof, I consider it of great value, as everything from the pen of so eminent a man must be, and do myself the honor of copying it:

COLONEL LOFTY'S CARD.

"GENTLEMEN, Editors of Atlanta 'Herald:'

"Returning home this evening, I have just read, with pleasure, your article in reply to the Augusta 'Chronicle and Sentinel.' Will you permit me, gentlemen, to add to it? If so, I would remark, that the first principle of human nature is, 'That every wrong must have its atonement.' Mr. Jefferson has said, either wisely or unwisely, 'That all men are, of right, born free and equal.' Mr. Blackstone has said, 'That the basis of all law, is the giving up of some right, for the better protection of others.'

"From these three axioms spring the Civil Code, and the Code of Honor, as well as the Constitution under which we live.

"Permit me, gentlemen, since I see so many condemning that of which they evidently know nothing, to hand you John Lyde Wilson's Code of Honor, and ask you to print it in your columns. I dare not add one word to the sentiments of that lofty gentleman, but submit if it be not true that the code is lofty, which bows the head of the most noble gentleman to the level of the lowest serf, if the gentleman has stooped to insult the serf. Permit me, also, to add, the duel is not the result of the code; it is the failure of the code, precisely as amputation is not the result of surgery, but its failure—the limb cannot be cured, we cut it off. Blood is so bad that a street-fight will result; parties are too much incensed; if they meet in the street, probably neither of them will be hurt, but innocent people will suffer. Well, the code takes these men out of the street; prevents their endangering others; leaves not their case and quarrel to themselves, but turns it over to two or four disinterested men of equal rank, who say what shall be done in the matter. If they cannot agree, they call a Board of Honor, which may consist of as many men as they see fit to select.

"Where lies, then, the difference between this law and the law of the land, save, that this gives men trial by their peers? The law of the land takes a jury; and we, of the modern day, alas, know what Courts of Justice are, and know how they are managed.

"And now, gentlemen, I submit to you a grief. Gentlemen, the principle of *meum et teum*. What is mine is mine, and is not yours. You have taken, within the last few days, the liberty of handling my name, and giving me and my friends, whom I had invited to join me in a pleasure excursion, a degree of notoriety exceedingly unpleasant to me and to them.

"I think, my friends, you owe it to me to withdraw both my name and theirs from public notice, simply upon the principle, that the dearest thing a man can have is his name and fame. 'What is mine is not thine; touch not thou it.' Believe me, my friends, modern journalism is in error upon that point. If not, however, as a right, as a favor—spare my name.

"And now, gentlemen, as you have touched my name, and that of my friends, I have a *right* to your columns for *reply*.

"I *beg* you, therefore, print me this one time and spare me in the future.

"I am, gentlemen, with profound respect, your sincere friend and most obedient servant,

"HERCULES D. LOFTY, M. D."

It will be seen, from this ably written card, that in this country a gentleman may now be compelled to fight a serf.

This liberal practice being established, many of the prejudices heretofore existing against the code in the minds of the ignorant, on account of its alleged exclusiveness, must be at once and forever dissipated. I was at some loss, however, to determine who were the serfs in this country, as at present organized, and Colonel Lofty being too distant from me to obtain his opinion, I consulted Doctor King upon the subject. He said, "that he supposed Colonel Lofty meant boat-hands when he alluded to serfs."

I give his opinion for what it is worth.

CHAPTER XXIX.

COLONEL LOFTY OPENS A CORRESPONDENCE WITH COLONEL HURD.

On the morning of the ninth of August, I was gratified by receiving the following pleasant note from Colonel Lofty, through the mail:

"ATLANTA, GA., August 7, 1873.
1:25, P.M.

"COLONEL GEORGE W. HURD.

"MY DEAR SIR:—You did me the honor to ask leave to call upon me unofficially at Neil's Landing, in Florida, on the twenty-third of July, at 3:30 P.M. You stated that your visit was an unofficial one. I replied, that I was glad to receive you at any time, and in any manner. You said you would ask me (unofficially), with a view to adjusting matters to suit our personal convenience, if the eighth of August would suit me for an answer to the note from Captain Porter, which I had just delivered to Major Woodson.

"A debate between you and myself followed, which referred to a Board of Honor two points, viz.:

"First. How much time was allowed you, or whether time at all?

"Second. Whether you should—in case time was allowed—address us a note, asking for the time, or announcing to us the time you took?

"The reply of the 'Board' was a note from Major James F. Woodson, addressed to Captain T. J. Porter, and handed me by a member of the 'Board,' Doctor Courtney. That note simply announced that Major Woodson would reply within the usual time.

"Now, Colonel, this may mean any time within forty-six days from the eighteenth of July, when I addressed my first note to Major Woodson, or it may refer to your 'unofficial' proposition of August eighth.

"Will you, my dear sir, in view of my personal affairs, enlighten me as to your time, so that I may have my personal affairs in readiness; otherwise, I shall be compelled to hold myself in constant readiness to move at a minute's warning from now until the morning of the third (3d) day of September, proximo.

"I shall do the latter, if you require it, but for my personal sake I would ask the charity of some definite understanding.

"I am, my dear Colonel, very respectfully,
"Your obedient servant,
"HERCULES D. LOFTY, M. D."

I answered this note as follows:

"OPELIKA, ALA., August 9, 1873.

"COLONEL HERCULES D. LOFTY.

"MY DEAR SIR:—Your favor of the seventh instant to hand. Contents noted. I regret not being able at present to give you definite information as to the intentions of the friend of Major Woodson. If I find I can do so, it will afford me pleasure to comply with your request.

"For fear of some future misconstruction, I feel it my duty to say, that my recollection does not concur with yours as to what took place between you and myself at Neil's Landing. I would at present call your attention to one point. You seem, from some reason, to count time from eighteenth of July, when, according to my recollection, the first and only note ever received from Captain Porter by Major Woodson, was dated twenty-third July, 1873, 3 P. M. While I have no idea that this date will ever be material, I deem it proper to refer to it in answer to your letter.

"I remain, sir, very respectfully,
"Your obedient servant,
"G. W. HURD."

On the twenty-second of August, I received the following letter, by mail, from Colonel Lofty:

"ATLANTA, GA., August 21, 1873.
NATIONAL HOTEL, 7:42, P. M.

"COLONEL G. W. HURD, Opelika, Ala.

"MY DEAR SIR:—I was absent when your favor of the eleventh, in reply to my note of the seventh instant, came to hand.

"I am sorry that 'your memory' of the occurrence at 'Neil's Landing,' differs from mine. I am quite sure mine serves me correctly. I shall regret if the 'different opinion' on your part continues, though, as you have failed to mention it to me, I do not know in what it consists. However, I have consulted my memory, and have referred my note to you to Doctor Courtney, and I am quite sure that the matter was as I had written you. Should you still, after considering the matter, continue in your same opinion, I fear we shall find our difference irreconcilable—in which case I can only say I am at your service, and humbly await your pleasure. I am sorry to tell you, that I cannot permit a count of time to run from the twenty-third of July.

"You are well aware that I commenced action on the eighteenth, and that I notified Major Woodson on that day, that I had a 'message for him;' and, as all subsequent delay arose from the action of your party, I cannot, in justice to my friend, permit advantage to be taken of it. There has been far too much delay, and, I regret to add, too much publicity, in this affair already; therefore, I am compelled to notify you, that my action will commence upon the morning of the third of September, 'proximo,' unless I shall hear from your party sooner. I shall await your pleasure at this point, and should I be compelled to move earlier, I will notify you, both by letter and telegram.

"Meanwhile, I am, Colonel,

"Your very obedient servant,

"HERCULES D. LOFTY, M. D."

To this letter I made the following reply:

"OPELIKA, ALA., August 22, 1873.

"COLONEL HERCULES D. LOFTY.

"MY DEAR SIR:—Your favor of the twenty-first instant is at hand. It would be very absurd for me to be offended with you, because my recollection of an 'unofficial' conversation does not happen to concur with yours. Being perfectly satisfied with my own recollection, I freely acknowledge your right to an equal confidence in yours.

"I concur with you in regretting the 'publicity,' which must, however, have been stopped by your card in the 'Herald.'

"As to your intimation of the course you intend to

pursue, in reference to Major Woodson, and the views you present as to his duty, I do not feel called upon to make any response, not representing him, as you are aware, in this matter. I presume that, on inspection, the correspondence between yourself, and Captain Porter, and Major Woodson, will speak for itself.

"I am, sir, very respectfully,

"Your obedient servant,

"G. W. Hurd."

CHAPTER XXX.

COLONEL LOFTY'S CORRESPONDENCE WITH COLONEL STRONG.

ON the 11th day of August, 1873, at the hour of 10 : 15 A. M., being busily engaged in my office, my attention was suddenly attracted by unusual sounds in the adjoining office of Colonel Strong. These words only caught my ear distinctly: *Pertinent!* IMPERTINENT PUPPY!! Then followed a crash, as if a blow had been struck. At once I rushed to the assistance of my friend, thinking him engaged in some, perhaps mortal, combat. He was alone; his chair upset; a letter in his hand; his face pale as death—always a sign, with him, of intense anger and excitement.

In answer to my hurried question as to what was the matter, he said: "*Read that!!* (handing me the letter which he held) and see what a fool your friend, Lofty, is. But before you read it, tell me, if you please, what the word pertinent means." I told him. "Exactly," said he, "that is what Webster says. Now, Colonel, I know you admire Colonel Lofty, and certainly your manners have improved, since you became acquainted with him. But if he has the impertinence to annoy me by writing about his 'pains and griefs,' occasioned by my asking him a pertinent question, I'll break a two-year-old hickory stick over his head."

Regretting, deeply, that my friend Colonel Strong

could not appreciate the sublime traits of character of my friend Colonel Lofty, I argued the matter with him, kindly, until he finally became calmer; and I read the admirable and feeling letter of Colonel Lofty, handed me by Colonel Strong, as follows:

"OFFICE AND SALES-ROOM OF PORTER & SMITH,

"Grocers and Commission Merchants, Manufacturers and Importers of Liquors, etc. Consignments and orders solicited.

"ATLANTA, Georgia, August 7, 1873.

"COLONEL F. T. STRONG, Editor 'Patriot,'

"MY DEAR SIR:—I have this moment seen Colonel Henry Y. Smith, who has just returned from Opelika, and tells me that you have returned from your Carolina trip.

"I did myself the honor to stop to see you at Opelika, on July the 28th, when on my way up from Columbus, Georgia, but had the mortification to find you gone.

"I hence, with pleasure, avail myself of this, the earliest moment, of addressing you. Permit me to express the hope, that your trip was a pleasant one.

"And now, my dear sir, for the '*res in gesta*.' Do you remember, my dear sir, the first visit that you and Colonel G. W. Hurd paid to me at the Rankin House, in Columbus, upon the 18th day of July? It was, I think, about 4:30 P. M. of that day, that you occasioned me a great grief.

"I think, my dear sir, that upon that occasion, without having been properly authenticated to me in writing, or otherwise, than by a verbal introduction, you permitted yourself to address to me a very pertinent question—so pertinent, indeed, was it, that I found myself unable to answer it, but told you that I would refer it to my friend, to whom it related. That I did so refer it, you must have been sure, for I brought my friend back with me and introduced him.

"You and Colonel Hurd then did me the honor to enter my room, where Colonel Hurd presented me a note. This note I was about to exhibit to my friend Doctor Courtney, when you permitted yourself, notwithstanding the sanctity of my room, and the pledge of the introduction I had just given you, to repeat, to Doctor Courtney, the very same question.

"So pertinent and so singular, Colonel, was your twice-repeated question, and so marked—I might almost say menacing—was your tone and manner, that I assure you, my dear sir, it occasioned severe pain and grief, both to myself and Doctor Courtney.

"My duties, as your host at the time, added to the very peculiar situation I was then occupying, precluded the possibility of my saying anything at that moment.

"I now approach you at the earliest moment practicable afterwards, and in doing so, I feel sure that it is only necessary to state to you the grief under which I have the mortification to suffer.

"Your earliest reply is respectfully requested.

"I am, my dear sir, with profound respect,

"Your most obedient servant,

"HERCULES D. LOFTY, M. D."

Colonel Strong answered this feeling letter as follows:

"OPELIKA, August 11, 1873.

"COLONEL HERCULES D. LOFTY.

"SIR:—Your polite communication of 7th instant, through the mail, has been received.

"I am not aware of having said anything, at the precise time to which you refer, that should have occasioned you either great 'pain' or 'grief.'

"I always studiously avoid asking other than 'pertinent questions.' And, if my recollection of the definition of the word 'pertinent' is correct, it seems to me you should not have been occasioned 'pain or grief,' by my propounding to you a 'pertinent question.' If my memory is not defective, the word 'pertinent' means, related to the subject, or matter, in hand; just to the purpose; adapted to the end proposed; apposite, etc.

"I am sir, respectfully,

"F. T. STRONG."

In vain did I attempt to induce Colonel Strong to use the words, "My Dear Sir," in addressing this note to Colonel Lofty, for I feared that his tender feeling would be wounded by being addressed as "*Sir*," and if so, the consequences might be terrible; but that great man kindly overlooked this important point, and answered as follows:

"ATLANTA, GA., August 21, 1873.
2:30 P. M.

"COLONEL F. T. STRONG, Editor, etc.

"MY DEAR SIR:—Your favor of the 11th instant I found waiting me on my return.

"Your reply, that you had no intention to pain Doctor Courtney, or myself, is entirely satisfactory to me.

"I have the honor to be, Colonel,

"Your obedient servant,

"HERCULES D. LOFTY, M. D."

CHAPTER XXXI.

MAJOR WOODSON SELECTS A SECOND.

On the 26th day of August, 1873, at 1:30 P. M., I left the city of Opelika; reached the town of Seal, upon the same day, at 5 P. M.; and while there, had the pleasure of meeting Major Woodson. He informed me, that he was ready to make his reply to the courteous note of Captain Porter.

But the question which now perplexed the Major was, whom, out of his numerous friends, he should select as his second. After the names of many had been canvassed, Major Woodson straightened himself in his chair, and bringing his right hand heavily upon the table near him, said: "Colonel, I shall request my friend, J. T. Hardy, to act for me."

I suggested, that Mr. Hardy had only arisen to the rank of Lieutenant in an artillery battalion—had even dropped that title since the close of the war. And, that, while Mr. Hardy was a man of undoubted honor, and a disciple of the code, yet he might be considered as wanting in that high polish and familiarity with it, which so distinguished Colonel Lofty; and, possibly, that gentleman might prefer dealing with a person more nearly approaching himself in rank and polish

Major Woodson looked me firmly in the eye, and said: "Colonel, I am not selecting a friend, in this matter, merely for the purpose of pleasing Colonel Lofty; what I mainly desire is, a man who suits myself, and one upon whom I can rely in any emergency. Now, Hardy stood by me at Baker's Creek, and through the siege of Vicksburg. I know him, and can depend on him; he shall act for me." At this time a messenger approached us, bringing letters to Major Woodson from the mail. I noticed a slight flush upon the Major's cheek, as he read one of these letters.

He presently handed it to me, remarking, "I suppose, Colonel, you will at least admit that your favorite assumes a good deal, in taking charge of both sides of this affair."

The letter which Major Woodson handed me, was as follows:

"ATLANTA, GA., August 24th, 1873.
"NATIONAL HOTEL, 2:20 P. M.

"MAJOR J. F. WOODSON:

"MY DEAR SIR:—I have just terminated a correspondence with Colonel Hurd, which, as it bears directly upon yourself, I feel it to be my duty to submit to you.

"You see, Major, that, either intentionally or otherwise, you failed to properly accredit Colonel Hurd to me. I consented, however, to receive your notes from his hands, because of his high character and standing; only taking the precaution to have each one properly authenticated, as having been delivered to me from you, together with the hour of delivery, as, save in one note, you had failed to fix the hour of writing.

"As Colonel Hurd now declines to hold the position of your friend, only as it may suit his convenience and taste, and as I have, certainly, waited a reasonable time for you to accredit some one to me, I ask you at once to name some friend, through whom the future correspondence, in relation to the affair between yourself and Captain Porter, may be conducted.

"As I have stated in my letter to Colonel Hurd, and for the reasons therein recited, I shall expect to receive your written reply to the note from Captain Porter—delivered by me to you, in person, at Neil's Landing, in the State of Florida, at 3 P. M. of July 23d—at least, by 10 A. M. of the 3d of September.

"In view of the manner in which I consider Colonel Hurd has trifled with me, I will expect, Major, your next messenger to be properly authenticated to me in writing.

"I shall await your pleasure at the National Hotel, in this city, unless some unforeseen circumstance should arise. Should I suddenly be required to move, I shall notify you, both by letter and telegram. Meantime, Major, I am, with profound respect,

"Your most obedient servant,

"HERCULES D. LOFTY, M. D."

After reading this letter, I remarked, "Colonel Lofty has more than once assured me, Major, that he took a deep interest in preserving not only your life, but your honor. And the advice he gives, is only wrung from him by that high-toned, chivalrous spirit, which cannot confine itself to a one-sided view of the question."

Next morning we took the train for Columbus, Georgia, and arrived there at 10:45 A. M. During the morning, Major Woodson requested me to read his reply to Colonel Lofty, which was as follows:

"COLUMBUS, GA., August 27th, 1873.

"COLONEL HERCULES D. LOFTY:

"SIR:—I have the honor to acknowledge the receipt of your communication of the 24th inst., enclosing a correspondence between yourself and Colonel Hurd, and advising me, that you would expect a reply, through some accredited friend, to Captain T. J. Porter's note of July 23d, by the 3d day of September, prox. Pardon me for saying, that I regret the correspondence between yourself and Colonel Hurd as unnecessary, and improper. He was my accredited agent to you, only in the correspondence which preceded the note of Captain Porter. Upon the receipt of that note, I became the custodian of my honor, and promised to reply 'within the usual time.'

"Any suggestions in the interim, such as your last note contains, you will again pardon me for saying I consider unkind.

"When I am ready, Colonel, I shall reply to Captain Porter; and in the mean time, I have the honor to be,

"Very respectfully,

"J. F. WOODSON."

Later in the day, Major Woodson had an interview with Mr. Hardy, who at once assured him, that nothing would give him more pleasure than to serve him, and so the question, as to who should act as Major Woodson's friend, was finally settled.

In a private interview with Mr. Hardy, I informed him, that Colonel Lofty was no ordinary man, and, as a duelist, had more experience than the gentlemen of Columbus, Opelika, Brownsville, and Seale, and the intervening country all put together, and besought him not only to consult the best living authorities, but to read up on dueling, and practice bowing and drinking whiskey. All this he promised to do, but seemed in no way affected by my account of Colonel Lofty. He smiled once or twice during the minute description which I gave of his many acts of daring, and quietly remarked, that he would like very well to see the man.

I felt great uneasiness about the effect of the selection of Major Woodson, and feared that the deliberate, and almost sarcastic, manner of Mr. Hardy might irritate Colonel Lofty.

CHAPTER XXXII.

COLONEL LOFTY WRITES TO COLONEL HURD.

On the 28th of August I arrived in Opelika, and, upon repairing to my office, found the following letter from Colonel Lofty awaiting me:

"ATLANTA, GA., August 23, 1873.
"8 P. M., National Hotel.

"COLONEL G. W. HURD:

"MY DEAR SIR:—Your prompt favor of 22d inst., in reply to mine of 21st, is to hand. While I am gratified, Colonel, at your promptness, you will forgive me if I say, that I am grieved at the lack of perspicuity in your reply.

"Let me deal with you frankly. I am not, like yourself, learned in the law and skilled to write words that convey a sound that soothes the mind and lulls to hope, but, at the period that should bring fruition, breaks the word of promise to the hope while keeping it to the ear, leaving dull despair and shameful dishonor to the waiting fool. I am, Colonel, but a plain, blunt man, unskilled in craft or wily tactics—a man who says exactly what he means, and means exactly what he says.

"Forgive me, then, if I find your note unsatisfactory. And believe me, in the name of truth, when I point out wherein it is unsatisfactory.

"In your letter of the 11th, you said, in reply to my

note of the 7th, that your memory of the occurrences at Neil's Landing differed from mine.

"Now, Colonel, I had written you upon the 7th what my memory was. If, therefore, your memory differs from mine, and you are not in error, either I had wilfully and deliberately lied, or I must have been a most egregious ass, to have written privately to you a thing or things of which I was not sure.

"This condition of things occurring to me, I was greatly distressed. I at once sent for Major Shelton and Doctor Courtney and consulted them. I referred to my letter to you, and have looked over all the papers in the case in order that my mind should come accurately to the point of our unofficial conversation. I gravely announce to you that I am unable, after all this care, to find a single error in my letter of 7th inst.

"I therefore respectfully ask, that you will at once specify distinctly wherein your memory differs from what I have written, as I assure you that I cannot consent to remain under a charge like that, though it be vaguely expressed and known only to you and myself.

"You regret, with me, the publicity this affair has obtained, and presume it was stopped by my card in the 'Herald.' I cannot permit you, Colonel, even in your own mind, to do my friends of the 'Herald' so much injustice. The 'Herald' only printed my card, and reprinted (as the cause of their action) the card of retraction of the 'Sun.'

"And this retraction of the 'Sun,' I am sure you know, cost me the pain of slapping the face and pulling the nose of Major De Soto, the editor. You know I had promised, both to your party and mine, that I would compel such a retraction, and you know I redeemed my word.

"You say as to the course you intend to pursue in reference to Major Woodson, and the views you present as to his duty, 'I do not feel called upon to make any response, not representing him, as you are aware. An inspection of the correspondence between yourself, Captain Porter, and Major Woodson, will speak for itself.' Well, Colonel, I have consulted, and will let it speak.

"I find from it that although you were never officially authenticated as the friend of Major Woodson, nevertheless you permitted yourself to bear every communication which I received from him.

"I own that you formally, but verbally, told me that in view of your connection with him, you could not proceed further in the case. I was therefore surprised (but agreeably so, as I was glad to find myself confronted by so courteous a gentleman) to find you on the boat with Major Woodson.

"After the delivery by me of Captain Porter's note to Major Woodson, you made me that informal visit, about which I have had the misfortune to find you differing from me in memory. It is, therefore, with trepidation that I remember you stated, that the Major would like to have his friend with him. When I expressed surprise, as you were there, you again reminded me of your relationship. I will not discuss this further with you, Colonel. I do not feel that 'the game is worth the candle.'

"I will only say to you plainly, as a plain man, that it seems to me you have trifled with me.

"As you now say distinctly, and in writing, that you are not the friend of Major Woodson, I shall annoy you no further about it, but at once address Major

Woodson, and request him to authenticate some friend to me with whom I may correspond.

"In conclusion, Colonel, I hope I shall not be thought going too far when I say that I trust, after your written disclaimer, that all active interference in this matter will cease, unless you intend fully to assume the responsibility of such action.

"I remain, Colonel, your very obedient servant,

"Humbly awaiting your pleasure,

"HERCULES D. LOFTY, M. D."

While deeply engaged in reading and pondering over this admirable letter, I was much irritated on being interrupted by the entrance of Charley Chip, to whom I remarked hastily: "Have you brought that miserable little tin account? I have certainly paid it, but call when I am at leisure, and I will pay it again, if I do not find your receipt. You see that I am engaged at present."

"No, sir," he replied in a more dignified manner than is usual with him, "the account is all right. No, sir, I called round, Colonel, to hand you this note from Colonel Lofty," and he presented me the following note:

"OPELIKA, August 28th, 1873.
"ADAMS HOUSE, 10 A. M.

"COLONEL G. W. HURD, *present en ville.*

"MY DEAR SIR:—Will you pardon me if I remind you, that up to this moment, my letter of the 23d remains unanswered. Allow me to respectfully inform you, that I am in this city, at the Adams House, where I will reside until I depart for Columbus, where I shall remain until the morning of the 3d of September. I shall reside at the Rankin House while there, and shall duly notify Major Woodson of my arrival.

"Permit me, Colonel, to call your attention again to my letter of the 23d inst., and allow me to renew my request, that you will state to me, in writing, wherein your memory differs from mine.

"Permit me to observe, that a charge so vague as this is very painful; and is one under which I cannot rest quietly with honor. It is one you should not make, without full specification and proof. I have now asked you no less than three times, to specify the charge you have made.

"Once more I beseech you; say distinctly and fully, in what your memory differs from mine.

"I humbly await your pleasure. With profound respect, Colonel,

"I am your most obedient servant,

"HERCULES D. LOFTY, M. D."

After reading this letter, I turned to young Chip solemnly, and said: "Charley, do you bear me this note from Colonel Lofty, as his friend or second?"

"No, sir! No, sir! Oh! no, Colonel; he asked me just to step in, and hand it to you. Do you want me to wait for an answer, Colonel?" he replied.

"No, Charley, you need not wait; tell Colonel Lofty, that I will honor myself by replying to his letter by mail. You may go now, Charley."

[*Exit* Charley.

CHAPTER XXXIII.

MR. HARDY MEETS COLONEL LOFTY.

PROFESSIONAL business occupied my attention during the twenty-eighth of August, and until 12 : 30 P. M., of the twenty-ninth. When I encountered Mr. Hardy stepping off the train from Columbus, he accosted and requested me to introduce him to Colonel Lofty. We repaired to the Adams House, and there met the Colonel.

After mutual profound salutations and expressions of pleasure at meeting, between Colonel Lofty and myself (during which Mr. Hardy stood by, perfectly unmoved, his eyes quietly directed upon Colonel Lofty,) I respectfully asked permission to introduce Mr. Hardy to Colonel Lofty, and, upon permission being granted, did so.

Colonel Lofty, with repeated salutations, expressed his great pleasure and delight at being honored by the acquaintance of Mr. Hardy. The latter, with a slight movement of his body, something like a bow, said, "He had wished for some days to see Colonel Lofty, and that he desired a private interview."

Colonel Lofty bowed profoundly and remarked, "That it would afford him great pleasure if Mr. Hardy would honor him by entering his humble apartment. I believe," he continued, "you are a brother of my old friend, Colonel O. L. Hardy?" Mr. Hardy replied,

"That Colonel O. L. Hardy was his brother." Upon my making a movement to retire, Mr. Hardy requested me to wait for him. "I will not detain you more than two minutes," he said.

I smiled, as they retired into Colonel Lofty's apartment, and looked at my watch, for I thought Mr. Hardy had reckoned without his host, in allowing only two minutes, when thirty or sixty would, in my opinion, be necessary—for I knew his business was to deliver a note, and, under the etiquette of the code, a note could not be delivered in less than thirty minutes, even if the whiskey part of the imposing ceremony was taken "*straight*."

Imagine, then, my astonishment when, at the expiration of one and one-half minutes, I saw both gentlemen returning. We walked into the passage of the hotel together, and had approached the flight of steps leading to the street, when Colonel Lofty, having left his hat and gloves, returned to search for them, and Hardy and myself stood together, he lounging negligently on the railing of the steps. I exclaimed, "It is not possible that you have delivered the note already?" "No," replied Hardy, "not exactly. You see, when we first went into the room, Colonel Lofty told me he would be honored and pleased, etc., to take the note as soon as we took whiskey. I told him that I always took business first and whiskey afterwards; then Colonel Lofty said, 'he wanted Mr. Count Bismarck and others to witness his taking the note.' It did not seem to me appropriate to have witnesses, especially as those he proposed, I knew, were not disciples of the code, and suggested the point to him, but he said, 'The way to make men admire the code and convert them to it was to let them see the practical workings of it,' and I, just to save time, told him to bring in his witnesses, and be quick about it, but it seems that we will have to tramp over the city to find these unconverted anti-duelists."

I replied, that it seemed to me unusual, but I supposed the overwhelming necessity of making converts to the code in these degenerate days might well excuse conducting the affair in a slightly irregular manner.

Colonel Lofty joining us, we walked up to Count Bismarck's store. I stopped at the door, but being requested by Colonel Lofty to assist in witnessing the important ceremony, entered, and we approached the Colonel, who stood in the middle of the store. (During the interview which followed, I could but be gratified at the evidently increased trade of my old friend Bismarck. His store was crowded.)

Mr. Hardy remarked: Colonel, have you now witnesses enough?

Lofty. Colonel Hardy (bow), I think, sir, that these gentlemen (bowing to first myself and then to Count Bismarck) will be sufficient. In some cases I require as many as four.

Hardy. Here is the note, then (handing it to Colonel Lofty).

Lofty. Colonel Hardy (bowing and taking the note lightly by the corner), I will now, sir, do myself the honor to take this note.

At this moment Mr. Hardy released his hold upon the note, not knowing that it was necessary, at this stage of the proceeding, for both gentlemen to hold the note up between them until the remarks of the recipient were concluded. Colonel Lofty not being prepared for this sudden withdrawal of the support from the opposite

"The Note was Quietly Resting on the Floor and no one Could Take it up."

[*Page* 157.]

corner of the missive, it unfortunately fell between them. Mr. Hardy leaned back against a pile of corn-sacks, glancing in a quiet, self-possessed manner alternately at the note, as it lay upon the floor, and at the face of Colonel Lofty, which had assumed a startled and surprised expression.

The question arose in my mind as to whose duty it was, under these most peculiar circumstances, to raise the note from the floor. I was willing to do it, but not being connected with the affair, except as a witness, was satisfied that it would be presumptuous in me to touch it. A second glance at Colonel Lofty's face showed me, that while that great duelist had probably never in his life been placed in so delicate and harassing a position, yet he was of opinion, that inasmuch as the delivery of the note and its reception, under the code etiquette, had not been completed, that it was the duty of Mr. Hardy to raise it from the floor, but that it would be indelicate in him, more especially as the point was novel and difficult, to express his views.

On glancing again at Mr. Hardy, I saw, from his nonchalant and satisfied expression of countenance, that he considered it no affair of his, and that he construed the words of Colonel Lofty, "I will now do myself the honor to take this note," accompanied by the actual taking a corner of it in his hand, as a delivery; and so the matter stood, and it is probable that a dead lock would here have been made, which might have stopped any further progress in the affair which I am recording, for the note was quietly resting on the floor, and no one could take it up—or at least each thought the other should do it—and there it must have remained had not our anti-dueling friend, Count Bismarck, who had been a few moments absent, waiting on a customer, returned and assisted the duel on its legs again by taking up the note and handing it to Colonel Lofty, saying: "Here is the note you dropped, Colonel," in such a quick impulsive way, that the Colonel had it actually in his hand before he was aware of what he was doing.

So solemn and impressive had been this scene, that trade had been suspended in Count Bismarck's store during its continuance. Not an article had been purchased (save and except two-and-a-half pounds of sugar, which Bismarck had himself weighed and sold to a poor woman), every tongue was still, every eye was turned alternately from the note to each of the living actors in the scene, every ear was attentive; even the casual passer-by on the side-walk paused with breath suspended and outstretched neck; and when, at last, by the action of the accommodating Bismarck, the note reached Colonel Lofty's hand, there was a long-drawn audible respiration of relief from the spectators, and trade went on—or at least as I at this moment turned my face to the spectators they turned theirs to the counters, and I heard inquiries as to the price of various articles.

Colonel Lofty now stood in his most erect position, with the note in his outstretched hand, and remarked: "Gentlemen, I am now placed in a most overwhelming and delicate position; never in the course of my experience have I seen such a serious accident occur as the unfortunate dropping of this note, after its delivery had been commenced, and before it had been completed. I am unable to say what would have been the result had not our friend, Mr. Count Bismarck, so courteously placed this note in my hands, acting, as it were, as the proxy, or agent of Mr. Hardy." And turning to Hardy, said, bowing low, "I suppose, Mr. Hardy, that you ratify and adopt the act of our friend, Mr. Count Bismarck, in completing the delivery of this note to me on your behalf?"

Hardy. I am not responsible for what Bismarck may do, or has done; I delivered you the note and you took it, and then let it fall, and he handed it to you. I see nothing wrong about the matter, and don't pretend to understand why you should stand and look at the note so long; I know but little about dueling.

Lofty. My dear Colonel Hardy (bow), it then seems you consider that you had completed the delivery of the note, when it unfortunately fell to the floor. That being the case, and inasmuch as I am now *de facto* in possession of the note, and as it would be discourteous in me to replace it on the floor, so as to place matters in *statu quo*, I will, in this peculiar and most interesting state of affairs, adopt your views. At the same time, feeling it my duty to say (pardon the expression), that your view is erroneous, and that I will never, in any future duel, be governed by this precedent.

Hardy. Colonel, I would be glad to get off on the first train, and if it suits your convenience to hurry matters, I would be pleased. If not, I will stay over.

Lofty. Colonel Hardy (bow), to suit your private interests, we will dispense with as much ceremony as possible in so important a matter; but, sir, it grieves me to do so.

Hardy. Then, Colonel, don't do it; I will stay over for the next train; just go on and talk as much as you wish.

Lofty. By no means, sir (bow). I will do myself the honor to read this note at once, without even waiting to be requested to do so (and he read as follows):

"COLUMBUS, GA., August 28th, 1873.

"CAPTAIN T. J. PORTER:

"SIR:—I regret if the delay, which I have found necessary in framing a reply to your note of 23d of July, may have caused you inconvenience. Your complaint is, that over my signature in the 'Sun' of 25th June, an advertisement appeared, containing cruel statements in regard to the character of your deceased relative. The greater portion of that article contains simply references to sworn testimony in a law case, to which I presume your note does not refer—"

At this point Colonel Lofty stopped reading, heaved a sigh, and said, "Major Hardy, it pains me exceedingly to decline to take this note, but it is my duty to do so; and Hercules Diogenes Lofty will do his duty, cost him what it may.

Hardy. Do you find anything discourteous or disrespectful in the note, Colonel Lofty?

Lofty. Mr. Hardy (bow), on the contrary, sir, I find it most courteously expressed and respectful in its terms. I will, with your permission, state the important reasons which prevent my receiving this most courteous note. Captain Porter had a fourth cousin, who is now dead, and being dead, it is a maxim, handed down to us from time immemorial, that his virtues, if he had any, must live after him, and be remembered, and his faults must be buried with him. Nothing can authorize any fault of a deceased person to be ever mentioned, or referred to, in any way. Major Woodson mentions sworn testimony, and presumes that Captain Porter's note does not refer to that portion of his article. Now, gentlemen, in the first place, no sworn testimony should ever be allowed in any case where it may affect injuriously the character of the dead. The bad character of the dead can never be discussed in any manner, or for any purpose; any living man or woman must be allowed to suffer or die, if need be, rather than assail the character of the dead. These principles are so well established under the code, that it is unnecessary to discuss them at length, and I will proceed now to show the gentlemen here present, what Major Woodson's note should have been, to be satisfactory to Captain Porter. First, then, he should have said——

Hardy. I would prefer, Colonel, your reducing your reasons for declining to take this note, to writing, to hearing your views about what character of note would be satisfactory to Captain Porter; but if you prefer talking longer, I will hear you through.

Lofty. Colonel Hardy (bow), I will do myself the honor, forthwith, to act as you desire.

And we walked into the back-room of Bismarck's store, and Colonel Lofty sat down to write, with his back towards a pail of fresh water standing near. Mr. Hardy raised a dipper full to his lips, remarking, "Bismarck, I'll take a drink." As the last word fell from Hardy's lips, Colonel Lofty arose, and in his most urbane manner, bowing profoundly, said, "Your suggestion, Mr. Hardy, is a most timely one; I will do myself the honor to join you." At this instant, his eye caught the dipper suspended in Hardy's hand, and he turned suddenly back to his writing, saying, "Thank you, Colonel, thank you; I never drink water. I consider it unhealthy, sir," and I saw a melancholy, disappointed look settle for a moment on his face.

In a few moments he turned again to Mr. Hardy,

remarking, "My dear sir, I am very much at a loss to know by what title to address you; will you do me the honor to inform me as to the title you prefer to be addressed by?"

Hardy. Certainly; just write me down a "field hand." I have no title.

Lofty. My dear sir (bowing), I beg that you will allow me to use some title; I assure you, sir, that if we should ever be compelled to print this most interesting correspondence, it will look much better.

Hardy. I never expect to have it printed; in fact, that is not my object; if we can settle the thing for these gentlemen fairly and honestly, I am willing, and if we cannot, then, I say, let them fight, and not print.

Lofty. My dear sir, your views do you great credit; but, as a personal favor to myself, I hope you will allow me to add the word Esquire after your name?

Hardy. I rather prefer being addressed as a "field hand," but, if it will gratify you, write me down Esquire.

And Colonel Lofty proceeded to write. When he was through, Bismarck stated that he had a great curiosity to hear the rest of Major Woodson's letter; "And I think," said he, "being called in as a witness, I am entitled to hear it all."

Lofty. If Mr. Hardy does not object (bow), I do not observe any particular objection. I deem it proper to state, however, that no matter what it may contain, the effect will be the same upon Hercules Diogenes Lofty.

Hardy. It is a matter of indifference to me; Colonel Lofty can do as he pleases.

Colonel Lofty thereupon read aloud the remainder of Major Woodson's letter, as follows:

"I confine my reply, therefore, to that portion which refers to his intercourse with Caroline Myers, and the circumstances connected with that transaction, embracing his disconnection with the Church. Permit me, in the outset, to state, that the article in question was written in reply to an anonymous correspondent of the 'Herald,' in defence of my client and kinsman, against whom the foulest charges had been preferred, pending his trial. The averments of that publication led me to an examination of all the facts in the case, and I was forced by it—reluctantly I confess—to state circumstances connected with your deceased relative which I would not have done, but for the attacks of this anonymous writer, and to disabuse the public mind of the prejudice sought to be engendered by it. These facts were derived from the very best authority, and their publication would never have been made had not the character of my information justified it. You will remark, also, that in the very letter of which you complain, I offer to correct any mistake which I may have made as to facts. Having premised this much then, I cannot do you the injustice to suppose, that in your request to me for the retraction of injurious reflections, you desire that I should retract anything which is true. I am unwilling to indulge any such violent presumption against any man whom I regard, and with whom I correspond, as a gentleman.

"Proceeding, then, upon this hypothesis, I have the honor to submit to your consideration the enclosed certificates, numbered from one to four,* from gentlemen of the highest respectability, and also some official records, covering your ground of complaint, the originals being

* See Appendix.

subject to your inspection at any time you may desire. I assure you that I regret the necessity of calling your attention to these facts, and would not do so if justice to myself did not require it.

"Additionally, I will state, that at the time I was first approached by your friend, Colonel Lofty, I was engaged in ferreting out a discrepancy in my charges, to which my attention had been called, and find that Mr. Smith, deceased, instead of being dropped, as stated by me, from the Church, had withdrawn at his own request. I cheerfully, therefore, make this correction, and any other in which you may be able to satisfy me that I have been misinformed.

"In conclusion, permit me to say, that you are correct in supposing that I did not intend *wantonly* to assail the dead, or *gratuitously* to wound the living. My discussion of the errors of the dead was forced upon me in the defense of my client; to the living, I intended no wound, gratuitous or otherwise. I meant simply, in the vindication of a cause to which I owed the most solemn obligations, to refute the assailants of my client with truth. Again trusting that I do not misconceive the purport of your request, and that this reply may be satisfactory to you, I transmit the same by the hands of my friend, J. T. Hardy, through whom any future communication may be made to me.

"I am, sir, respectfully,

"Your obedient servant,

"J. F. WOODSON."

CHAPTER XXXIV.

AT THE RUBY.

WHEN Colonel Lofty finished reading the letter of Major Woodson, he said: "Gentlemen (bowing), the reading of that letter has made me very thirsty. May I indulge the hope, that you will honor me by drinking with me?" We bowed an assent, and he continued: "There are four of us, and it will cost one dollar. I have plenty of money, but allow me to remark, that I would not live, permanently, in any city where drinks are twenty-five cents; not that there is any difference between fifteen cents and twenty-five cents, but I consider it an imposition upon the gentlemen of our country." He then turned, and politely requested one, of a number of persons who had approached us, to copy the note he had written to Mr. Hardy, which request was acceded to with great alacrity.

Then we solemnly and silently marched down to the Ruby; for solemnity and secrecy are necessities in dueling, now, when the laws of the land are so much opposed to the system.

On arriving at the Ruby, each ordered his favorite beverage; then we bowed, and clinked our glasses together, and drank with the reverberation of the martial sound, and bowed again, lighted our cigars, and returned, using the utmost prudence and solemnity, to prevent any one from suspecting that a duel was contemplated. To effect this object more certainly, Colonel Lofty and Mr. Hardy walked together, so that the people should see they were friendly. Count Bismarck and myself followed, arm in arm. As we walked thus, he whispered: "Colonel Hurd, I am opposed to dueling on principle, and know but little about it; but the only part of it which I do understand, I like very much. That is the drinking part."

When we arrived at Bismarck's store, the copy of Colonel Lofty's note was complete. The original was delivered to Mr. Hardy; but, I regret to say, that the beautiful ceremony of delivery was shortened by Mr. Hardy's quietly, but firmly, seizing with an iron grasp the note, as soon as it was within his reach—it being held by Colonel Lofty, suspended with his thumb and forefinger by its extreme corner—saying, "All right, Colonel; you see that I never drop a note when it is handed to me."

He then slowly read the note, as follows:

"OPELIKA, ALA., August 29th, 1873.
"Bismarck's store, back-room, 2 P. M.

"J. T. HARDY, ESQ., *present en ville.*

"MY DEAR SIR:—I hope you will pardon my returning to you the letter and enclosed certificates from Major Woodson, addressed to Captain Porter, which you have to-day presented to me.

"I cannot consent to bear this letter to Captain Porter, as I do not conceive that it in any way touches the ground of his complaint against Major Woodson.

"Captain Porter cannot consent to any investigation of the memory of the dead, whose faults, if they had any, should be sacred; their good deeds, if any they have done, should live after them.

"Be pleased to refer to the verbiage of the note of Captain Porter, to which I have referred.

"If you should desire it, I will, at any time, write what will be satisfactory to Captain Porter.

"I am, dear sir, with profound respect,

"Your most obedient servant,

"HERCULES D. LOFTY, M. D."

After reading this note, Mr. Hardy quietly, and without asking permission, placed it in his pocket, together with the note of Major Woodson, and we repaired again to the Ruby, using the same precautions as on our first visit. Arriving there, I was pleased to see the trade of that bar on the increase so much, so that we could not approach the counter, and time being precious, Colonel Lofty, with a profound bow, requested us to honor him by holding a conference, and, upon an assent being given, he led the way to the side of the room, opposite the bar counter, and, at least, fifteen feet distant from it, so that our conference should be strictly private. In fact, we were so situated that, although plainly in view, we would not necessarily be heard by the patrons of the bar amid the clink of glasses, unless they deliberately chose to listen, which no gentleman would do, under such circumstances; and it was to be presumed that none but gentlemen entered the Ruby. Colonel Lofty turned, facing us and the bar, and said: "Gentlemen (bowing), I wish, with your kind permission, to do myself the honor of making a few remarks. My course in declining to bear the note of Major Woodson, may seem to you singular and unprecedented; but, gentlemen, I assure you, that in four of the most important affairs I ever conducted, this precise point arose, and I decided it in the same way. And I assure you, Mr. Hardy, that if you feel aggrieved by my course, I will only be too happy to meet you. (At this moment, the eyes of Mr. Hardy were quietly raised to those of Colonel Lofty, and remained fixed upon them. After a momentary pause, the Colonel continued:) At the same time, I feel it but just to myself to state that no offense was intended. I acted as I did, simply because I knew I was right. It was Captain Porter's duty to protect the character of his deceased cousin. No other man could do it. Some persons may contend, that the duty devolved upon the brothers or the sons of the deceased, and this might be a plausible point, were it not for the fact that Captain Porter's first name, Tom, is the same as that of his cousin; therefore, the duty of cleansing his cousin's memory from all stain more particularly devolves upon him, and he having undertaken this important task under my direction, Hercules Diogenes Lofty will not permit him to have that relative's faults mentioned, and, to satisfy him, Major Woodson must write a different kind of note.

Now you, Colonel Hardy (I hope you will permit me to address you as Colonel? it is more pleasant and convenient to me), have admitted that you are not very familiar with dueling, and nothing will give me more pleasure than to give you any advice you need in carrying on this affair; and you may trust in my judgment implicitly; and when you desire it, let me know, and I will give you the draft of a note, which Major Woodson can copy in his own hand, and which, I assure you, will be satisfactory to Captain Porter. And allow me to remark, Colonel Hardy, that nothing is more probable, than that you and myself will be compelled to fight, before we satisfactorily wind up this affair. It almost invariably happens, in the affairs which I do myself the honor to conduct, that I fight and often kill the opposing second, for some difference of opinion from me; and, therefore, if we should meet, I assure you in advance, that my feeling to you will be friendly.

Hardy. Colonel Lofty, while I think we might have found a more appropriate place to discuss matters, yet, since you have broached the subject here, I will reply to you by saying, first, that while I know but little about the code, I take the liberty of differing with you on every proposition you have laid down, and every position you have taken, since my acquaintance with you began.

I think you should have taken this note to Captain Porter, and if he was not satisfied with it, let *him* say so. I do not see that you have any right to presume that Major Woodson is so anxious to write a note satisfactory to Captain Porter, as to allow you to write his reply.

As to the character of the dead, I do not consider that more sacred than the character of the living, and in some cases it may be attacked.

As to your habit of fighting the seconds opposed to you, for differing with you, I have nothing to say (not having been present at any of your fights), except to let you know, that at any time you wish me to fight for differing with you, or for anything else, just let me know in plain English, so that I can understand you, and I'll give you all the satisfaction you desire. And now, Colonel, as we have come to a full understanding of our respective positions, we had better take our drinks, and not talk any more about fighting, until we get fixed to do a little of it.

Lofty. My dear Colonel Hardy (bow), it gives me untold pleasure to have formed the acquaintance of such a gentleman as yourself. And if we ever meet on the field of honor (which I do not say will be absolutely necessary), we will take a drink together, just before we fire, and, in the mean time, we will take one now, as you propose.

And we drank with the usual ceremonies. And then Colonel Lofty turned to me, saying, "Colonel Hurd, will you, sir, do me the honor of granting a private interview?"

I replied, "Colonel, it pains me beyond measure, to be compelled to ask you to excuse me from honoring myself by complying with your polite request. Please be so kind as to remember, that we differed in our recollection of what once took place between us in a private interview. I hope you will agree with me, as to the propriety of not placing ourselves in a position where another difference might occur, until the last is satisfactorily settled.

Lofty. Colonel Hurd (bow), considering the most remarkable circumstances by which we are surrounded, I think your excuse is sufficient; but, allow me to remark, that I am awaiting, most anxiously, your reply to my letter of 23d instant. (And then we smoked, and bowed, and parted, and Mr. Hardy took the 3.10 P. M. train for Columbus.)

CHAPTER XXXV.

CORRESPONDENCE BETWEEN COLONEL LOFTY AND COLONEL HURD PROGRESSES.

At 5 : 20 P. M. of the 29th of August I was sitting in my office, with Colonel Lofty's letter of 23d instant, and my answer to it, which I had just completed, lying before me. On looking up, after signing my name, I was surprised to see, standing directly in front of me, Charley Chip, dressed in his best suit, a slight twitching perceptible about the corners of his mouth.

With an air of importance I had never seen him exhibit before, he said, holding his hat before him, with both hands: "Colonel, I've got another note for you, sir, from Colonel Lofty."

"Ah! what is it about, Charley?" I replied.

"It's just a copy of the last note I brought you, Colonel, except Colonel Lofty has put my name in it at the bottom" (straightening himself with pardonable pride).

"Am I to understand, Charley, that you bring this note as Colonel Lofty's friend?"

"Yes, sir; yes, sir, I reckon so, Colonel," he said in an excited and tremulous manner.

On hearing this reply, I rose from my seat slowly and stood erect, assuming all the solemnity and dignity which I had acquired from Colonel Lofty, and looking down on him said:

"Mr. Chip, I shall be compelled to pain myself and you by declining to receive the note you bear. You are entitled, under the code, to have my reasons for declining in writing, and I will proceed at once to give them to you, unless you prefer to take the night to reflect upon this momentous subject, which may be the turning point in your life."

He replied, "Yes, sir, if you please, sir; I would like to take to-night to think about it; please let me wait until morning, sir." I said, "Yes, Charley, you may wait until to-morrow, and then present the note if you wish to do so."

"Thank you, Colonel, thank you, sir; I never worked at such a business as this before," he replied. (Exit Charley Chip.)

Thereupon I mailed my letter to Colonel Lofty, which was as follows:

"OPELIKA, August 29, 1873, 4 P. M.

"COLONEL HERCULES D. LOFTY:

"MY DEAR SIR:—Your favor of the 23d reached me only yesterday. About the same time I received a note from you, sent by a messenger, asking a reply to the same. I stated to your messenger that I would send you a reply by mail, at my earliest convenience.

"First, then, I have made no charge against you, and a re-perusal of my notes will show it.

"Second, my memory differed from yours, and I mentioned that fact to you.

"I am surprised that you should, for a moment, suppose that it was necessary, to sustain your honor, that my memory should concur with yours in every particular. But to the point. You wish to know wherein my memory differs. In complying with your request, I find it more convenient to state, as nearly as I can, what I remember of our conversation, and leave you to judge of the difference.

"On the evening of 23d July, at 3 : 30 P. M., I called on you, and upon your bowing most profoundly, I stated that my call was informal, and the following conversation ensued :

"*Colonel Lofty* (with a low bow). It gives me pleasure, sir, to see you at any time and in any manner.

"*Hurd* (with bow equally low). Allow me, sir, to express an equal pleasure in seeing you.

"*Lofty* (bow as before). Will you do me the honor, sir, to be seated?

"*Hurd* (bow as before). I will do myself the honor of sitting as you request.

"*Hurd* (on taking his seat). Colonel, will you permit me to inquire, where you can be found on or about the 8th day of August? I take the liberty of inquiring because Major Woodson's selected friend is not here, and I do not think that his reply will be ready before that time.

"*Lofty*. Major Woodson has certainly the right, under the code, to double the time taken by Captain Porter, but it would suit my convenience better if Major Woodson could reply before my return to Atlanta. You are, perhaps, aware, Colonel, that my principal, Captain Porter, is a wealthy man, and I know that Major Woodson is also wealthy, but you and myself are both poor, and it comes very hard on us to have to make two trips here. It is so expensive.

"*Hurd*. I have no doubt that Major Woodson and his friend will do anything that they can, consistently with their own convenience, to avoid putting you to expense or inconvenience, and I would suggest, that it is possible, before we part on our return, after Major Woodson consults with his friend, that some arrangement may be made to suit the mutual convenience of all parties.

"*Lofty.* Would you object, Colonel, to indicating to me what weapon Major Woodson will be likely to select, if the affair progresses to that point?

"*Hurd.* I am not at liberty to give you the information you desire, and allow me to suggest, that it is the duty of seconds to exhaust every effort to prevent a collision, before selecting weapons—is it necessary, therefore, to calculate beforehand that their efforts will be fruitless? But your experience is so much more extended than mine, that I feel a great delicacy in making any suggestion.

"*Lofty* (rising with profound bow). Yes, Colonel, I have been engaged in forty-two affairs of honor, as principal and second, and I concur with you fully in your suggestions. It is the duty of a second to prevent a resort to arms, if possible. I recollect in one of the first duels I ever fought, I came very near losing my life by having a fool for a second. He allowed me to fight the best swordsman in Europe with a rapier. I, at that time, was not so proficient as I am now in the use of that weapon, and considered my life as good as lost, but met my antagonist fearlessly, and, after parrying a few of his thrusts, was compelled to allow him to pass his sword entirely through my stomach, the point coming out at my backbone. As I stood thus transfixed, it occurred to my mind to do an act which I have never heard of being equalled, before or since. I, with

"I came very near loosing my Life by having a Fool for a Second." [Page 174.]

my left hand, with remarkable presence of mind, coolness, and firmness, seized my adversary's blade, holding it so firmly, that he could neither turn it in me or pull it out, and in that position, plunged my sword entirely through my adversary's left breast up to the hilt, just one inch and a half above his heart; and what is remarkable, is, that we both recovered—(and, thereupon, you removed a portion of your clothing and pointed to the spot). Nothing was said in this conversation, that I recollect, about a board of honor, or any note from Major Woodson. (Later in the evening we had another conversation, which I do not give, as your letter refers only to the one at 3:30 P. M.)

"Why you should have to consult Messrs. Shelton or Courtney, or the correspondence, to refresh your mind, I am unable to conceive, for neither of the gentlemen were present at the 3:30 conversation, and none of the correspondence refers to it.

"I only give my best recollection, and while on many points it may be incorrect, permit me to state that yours may not be any more reliable than mine. Of course, no gentleman would intentionally state an untruth, but it is rare for men's memories to concur exactly. Take, for instance, your statement to me in your note, that you had pulled the nose and slapped the face of Major De Soto. Now, I am assured that Major De Soto, who is a high-toned, truthful man, has no recollection of such an occurrence.

"You surprise me by alluding, in your letter, to the possibility of your being an 'egregious ass,' and a 'waiting fool.' I am sure that no expression, in either of my notes, could be construed as making such a charge, and if you so construe my writing, I beg to assure you I had no such intention.

"You assure me of the pleasure you experienced in my going on the boat. Allow me, sir, in return, to assure you that never have I experienced more pleasure and enjoyment than on that trip, for which I am mainly indebted to yourself, and I assure you that I am not alone when I state that your urbanity and courtesy were unsurpassed. In fact, on this point, I think the memory of all parties concurs.

"And now, Colonel, I assume the honor of signing my name, with profound respect,

"Your most obedient servant,

"GEO. W. HURD."

On the 30th, at 12 M., I was deeply gratified by receiving, through the mail, the following admirable and characteristic letter from Colonel Lofty:

"OPELIKA, ALA., August 30, 1873.
"ADAMS HOUSE, Room 6, 10 A. M.

"COLONEL GEO. W. HURD, *present en ville.*

"MY DEAR SIR:—Your most extraordinary letter of this A. M., in reply to mine of 23d instant, is to hand. Its contents are so strange and voluminous that I cannot say they are as yet carefully noted. I will reply in due time.

"I am, Colonel, most truly,

"Your friend and obedient servant,

"HERCULES D. LOFTY, M. D."

CHAPTER XXXVI.

CORRESPONDENCE BETWEEN COLONEL LOFTY AND MR. HARDY.

At 1:05 P. M., of 30th of August, I entered the train for Columbus, and arrived in that city at 3:35 P. M. of the same day, and found there Major Woodson and Mr. Hardy, the latter quite unwell, but of opinion that he would recover by the morrow.

On the 1st day of September, 1873, Colonel Lofty, accompanied by Major Shelton, Captain Carter, and Captain Wilson, arrived in the city. Colonel Lofty occupying room 10 at the Rankin House, and the other gentlemen of his party occupying rooms 12 and 14 adjoining.

At 3:45 P. M. Mr. Hardy handed to Colonel Lofty the following note from himself:

"COLUMBUS, GA., August 30, 1873, 3 P. M.

"COLONEL H. D. LOFTY.

"DEAR SIR:—Your note of the 29th instant is before me, in which you say, 'I cannot consent to bear this letter to Captain Porter, as I do not conceive that it in any way touches the ground of his complaint,' and in which you are pleased to refer me to the verbiage of the note of Captain Porter.

"I have, at your suggestion, examined the note of

Captain Porter (which I had not seen until this moment), to ascertain whether or not Major Woodson's note of the 28th August did touch the ground of his complaint, and on that examination I have concluded that it does touch the ground of complaint, mentioned in Captain Porter's note.

"I am, Colonel, very respectfully,
"Your obedient servant,
"J. T. HARDY."

What occurred at this interview, except the bare delivery of the note, I regret not being able to state, for Mr. Hardy, continuing quite unwell, failed to give me the particulars.

At 5 P. M. Colonel Lofty sent, by his friend Captain Carter, the following note to Mr. Hardy:

"COLUMBUS, GA., RANKIN HOUSE, ROOM 10,
"September 1st, 1873, 4:45 P. M.

"J. T. HARDY, ESQ., *present en vil'e.*

"MY DEAR SIR:—Your favor of August 30, delivered to me by yourself, about 3:30 P. M., is before me. You quote my language, and say that I said, 'I cannot consent to bear this letter to Captain Porter, as I do not conceive that it in any way touches the ground of his complaint.' In reply, you say, 'I have, at your suggestion, examined the note of Captain Porter, to ascertain whether or not Major Woodson's note, of 28th August, did touch the ground of his complaint; and, on that examination, I have concluded that it does touch the ground of complaint mentioned in Captain Porter's note.' My dear sir, the issue you make with me is a very peculiar and personal one. I have taken the trouble to send for Captain Porter, who has come to me, and fully sustains me in what I have done. I now have the honor to notify Major Woodson that his letter is unsatisfactory to Captain Porter. As to the difference of opinion between you and myself, I have the pleasure to say, that Captain Porter and myself will leave this, at 8 A. M. of to-morrow, for the ground to which Major Woodson once invited us, and both Captain Porter and Major Woodson, as well as you and myself, can continue our correspondence. For the original matter, I will say, once more, that Major Woodson's reply is unsatisfactory to Captain Porter, as well as to myself; and hence, should I not hear further, my action upon the 3d instant will be the same as if no reply had been made. My friend, Captain J. C. Carter, whom I beg to introduce to you, will hand you this, and will bear me any reply you may choose to make.

"I am, sir,

"Your obedient servant,

"HERCULES D. LOFTY, M. D."

Again, I am only able to express regret at my inability to state what took place at the moment of delivery of this important note, having only heard some of the concluding remarks on the subject, as follows:

Hardy. It will be inconvenient, Captain Carter, for me to answer this note before twelve to-morrow.

Carter. The hour you name will exactly suit Colonel Lofty's convenience; he is residing at the Rankin House, room number ten. I reside in number twelve, where you or your friend can find me. We would be greatly obliged, Colonel Hardy, if your reply is made at as early an hour as convenient, for our expenses are very heavy.

Hardy. My reply will be made at as early an hour as possible.

And they bowed, and parted.

CHAPTER XXXVII.

COLONEL HURD REFUSES TO RECEIVE A NOTE FROM COLONEL LOFTY.

AT the hour of 6:30 P. M., on the 1st day of September, 1873, I was sitting in General Rock's office, quietly smoking a cigar, and conversing with my friend, Doctor Jones. Mr. Hardy was lying on a couch, suffering from a severe headache.

Our conversation was interrupted by the entrance of Captain Carter, Major Shelton, and Captain Wilson.

Major Shelton greeted me cordially, and introduced me to Captain Carter and Captain Wilson. Captain Carter then requested a private interview, and he and myself retired into another room, where he presented to me the following note:

"COLUMBUS, GA., RANKIN HOUSE, ROOM 10.
"September 1st, 1873, 6:10 P. M.

"COLONEL GEORGE W. HURD, *present en ville.*

"MY DEAR SIR:—Your polite and courteous letter, of 29th instant, reached me on the morning of the 30th. I have not, as yet, quite mastered its contents, as business of overwhelming importance has not allowed me to devote more than one half of my time to it. When I am at leisure I will honor myself by replying. I will only say now, that I think you omitted one bow I made you. To this note I wish no answer. It will be handed to you by Captain Carter, Major Shelton, and Captain Wilson, who are authorized to act for me.

"I remain, my dear Colonel, with profound respect,

"Your obedient servant,

"HERCULES D. LOFTY, M. D."

It pained me exceedingly to be obliged to refuse to receive this elegant note, but honor compelled me to do so, and I stated my reasons to Captain Carter, in writing, as follows:

"COLUMBUS, GA., GENERAL ROCK'S OFFICE.
"September 1st, 1873, 7:11 P. M.

"CAPTAIN J. C. CARTER.

"DEAR SIR:—I respectfully decline to receive the note you bear from Colonel Lofty, because, first, I am informed by it that no reply is desired; second, Colonel Lofty has seen fit to open and conduct his correspondence with me on this subject by mail, and I prefer not carrying on, simultaneously, a double correspondence on the same subject, through two distinct channels. Besides the above, other important reasons exist, which prevent my reception of this note.

"I am, sir, very respectfully,

"G. W. HURD."

This note was delivered by me to Captain Carter in person, in the presence of the gentlemen who accompanied him, and of those who were with me on his arrival.

Now, although Colonel Lofty was not present at the time of the presentation of his note to me by Captain Carter, yet he has kindly reduced to writing his recollection of that occurrence, in a letter to me of September 17th, 1873, copied in chapter XLI. And the question which has agitated my mind, ever since I commenced this chapter, is, whether it would be courteous in me to give my recollection of that occurrence, it being different from that of Colonel Lofty

After calm deliberation, when I reflect on how much my readers and myself owe to Colonel Lofty, I feel that it is but due to him that his recollection of this occurrence should stand as he has written it, and that the harmony of this work may not be marred by contradictions.

CHAPTER XXXVIII.

MR. HARDY, FROM HIS SICK-BED, CONTINUES TO CORRESPOND WITH COLONEL LOFTY.

On the morning of the 2d of September the city was rife with reports of Mr. Hardy's alarming illness. The best physicians hurried to his bedside. Major Woodson and myself, of course, procured a carriage, rode out to see, and found him delirious with a raging fever. His physicians reported that he might be better or worse in a few days.

Ah! but for the present, what could be done? Colonel Lofty's note must be answered by 12 M. of this day. It was now 9 A. M. Patiently we waited by his bedside, hoping for a lucid interval; notwithstanding the surgeon's opinion, we hoped for it, and, finally, it came at 11:30 A. M. He was barely able to address two brief notes; and then he rolled again upon his bed of pain.

Our horses were harnessed, and, at 11:45, we were in the city; a friend was selected to informally deliver the notes; and they reached Captain Carter's hands at 11:55 A. M., in ample time. They read as follows:

"At Home, September 2, 1873.

"Captain J. C. Carter.

"Dear Sir:—I am to-day confined to my bed by a violent attack of sickness, which compels me to transmit you my reply to the note of Colonel Lofty, of yesterday, by the hands of a gentleman who has kindly consented to bear it. Please hand the same to Colonel Lofty, and oblige,

"Very respectfully,

"J. T. HARDY."

"COLUMBUS, GA., September 2, 1873.

"COLONEL HERCULES D. LOFTY.

"DEAR SIR:—Your note of yesterday was received by the hands of Captain J. C. Carter, in which you say that the issue I make with you is a very peculiar and personal one. I cannot, however, conceive that the issue is either peculiar or personal—it certainly was not designed to be so. Upon the contrary, I thought, and still think, that Major Woodson's letter, of the 28th ult., did touch the ground of Captain Porter's complaint, in his letter of the 23d of July. This, then, is the issue between us. Captain Porter, it appears, sustains your views—my own are unchanged. Now, in this state of affairs, when gentlemen thus honestly differ, I suggest, for your consideration, that the point be decided by gentlemen chosen, to whom the same may be referred.

"I am, sir, respectfully,

"J. T. HARDY."

At 3:40 P. M. Captain Carter called on Mr. Hardy, and found him still prostrate, and handed him a note from Colonel Lofty. Mr. Hardy being unable to raise himself in his bed, was also unable to bow upon the reception of this note, but this important part of the ceremony of delivery was courteously waived by Captain Carter, as was also that of reading the note and the drinking, on account of the illness of Mr. Hardy; the ceremony of delivery, being greatly shortened thereby, occupied less than three minutes. When it ended, Captain Carter entered his buggy, which stood ready at Mr. Hardy's gate, and drove rapidly back toward the city. The note which Captain Carter thus left on the bed of Mr. Hardy was in the following words:

"COLUMBUS, GA., RANKIN HOUSE, ROOM NO. 10.
"September 2, 1873, 2 : 30 P. M.

"COLONEL J. T. HARDY.

"MY DEAR SIR:—Your reply of this instant, delivered, 'informally,' to Captain J. C. Carter, by Doctor D. W. Jones, lies before me.

"You say, 'I cannot, however, conceive that the issue is either peculiar or personal—it certainly was not designed to be so.'

"My dear sir, this would certainly be as full an apology as I could ask of you if you had not, I have no doubt unthoughtedly, added a reiteration of the point of difference. You do me the unkindness to say, 'I thought, and still think, that Major Woodson's note, of the 28th ultimo, did touch the ground of Captain Porter's complaint, in his letter of 23d July. Captain Porter, it appears, sustains your views. My own are unchanged. Now, in this state of affairs, when gentlemen thus honestly differ, I suggest, for your consideration, that the point between us be decided by gentlemen chosen, to whom the same may be referred.'

"My dear sir, let me understand you distinctly. I understand that you wish to refer the point between you and myself to a board of gentlemen. If so, I consent. But if you mean with regard to Captain Porter and Major Woodson, I have to inform you, that three times I have submitted to boards of honor. Once, the gentlemen proposing, concluded that they could not act (that was the second one, and at Eufaula). The first and the last were here; and, I regret to say, that Major Woodson quibbled in each case, and the boards therefore failed.

"I regret to be so plain, but you leave me no alternative. I make this assertion with all its responsibilities. I therefore respectfully decline to have any further delay in Captain Porter's matters.

"I am going to the point I indicated at 4 P. M. of this day. If I go, and return without a satisfactory answer, I shall certainly act as I have four times before notified your party.

"With regard to our personal difference, if that is what you wish to refer, I can only say, I will refer it or not, as you please. If that be the point, I name Doctor Courtney and Major Shelton as my party. Please notify me of yours, and the time of meeting, which I leave to you, provided it be after my return from the trip upon which I am starting. Or it may, if you like, take place upon the boat as we journey.

"I am, my dear sir,

"Most truly your obedient servant to command,

"HERCULES D. LOFTY, M. D."

CHAPTER XXXIX.

A MASTERLY MANŒUVRE.

At 5 P. M., on the 2d of September, Major Woodson and myself were sitting with Doctor Wyatt, in front of his office, enjoying some very fine Havana cigars, when a mounted messenger dashed up to us, and handed Major Woodson a note from Mr. Hardy, inclosing the letter from Colonel Lofty to himself, of 2 : 30 P. M., copied in last chapter.

By immediate inquiry at the depot and hotel, we ascertained that Colonel Lofty and his party had taken the 4 P. M. train, to connect with the boat at Eufaula.

This sudden and unexpected movement, of course, produced considerable excitement, not only among the friends of Major Woodson, but throughout the city; for the secrecy and solemnity, necessarily observed, had awakened curiosity and inquiry; and, it being impossible for a gentleman to "tell an untruth, or to prevaricate in the slightest degree," everything seemed to be known, except some minor details.

Many and varied were the expressions of opinion upon the subject of this last movement of Colonel Lofty.

Some considered Major Woodson's honor as lost, and blamed Colonel Lofty for robbing him of it, without allowing him a possible chance to defend it. Others went so far as to say, that Colonel Lofty was afraid a fight would ensue, if Major Woodson had been allowed an opportunity of accompanying this party to Neil's Landing, and that he had executed this stratagem to avoid one.

All did the chivalrous and considerate gentleman most grievous injustice, and attributed to him motives which never for a moment could have been harbored in that gallant breast.

But who could expect the opponents of dueling, and those but slightly acquainted with it, to appreciate or understand that delicate sense of honor which actuates a man who makes it his life-long study, and sleeps with a copy of the code under his head?

To my mind (owing to my intimate association with him), the motive of Colonel Lofty was commendable. His action filled me with admiration. I now understood his often repeated remarks to myself, that he desired to save not only the life but the honor of Major Woodson. At the time they were made, they seemed to me mysterious, but now all was clear. By this admirable manœuvre, Colonel Lofty protected Major Woodson's honor, and prevented any peril to his life. It being impossible for Major Woodson to go to Neil's Landing, on account, 1st, of the illness of his second, who could not, under any circumstances, be left; 2d, because no spot had been agreed on; 3d, because of the physical impossibility of reaching there; his honor, of course, remained untarnished; and no blame, under the code, could attach to a gentleman for not doing that which was impossible, and which honor and self-respect prohibited him from doing.

At the same time this eminent tactician had been equally careful to preserve, not only the life and honor of his principal, but that of his entire family, for he took with him four distinguished gentlemen, besides himself, to give a certificate to that effect.

And a publication of almost all the correspondence in the "Atlanta Herald," cleared the last vestige of a stain from the honor of Captain Porter.

Thus, by a single effort of that master mind, the lives of all were saved, the honor of all preserved.

The attempt which I made to impress this practical solution of the action of Colonel Lofty, upon the friends of Major Woodson, was without avail. They would not hear me, and hence I have written my views of the motives which actuated this great duelist, that future generations may do justice to his memory, and imitate his example.

Not having accompanied Colonel Lofty in this second trip to Neil's Landing, I am unable to state accurately what occurred there; but, through the kindness of the Colonel in allowing the newspapers to print some of the correspondence and circumstances in this remarkable case, I am enabled to give my readers the following copy of the certificate, which had the effect of clearing the honor of Captain Porter from all stain:

"Neil's Landing, Fla., 6 p. m., Sept. 6, 1873.

"Captain T. J. Porter.

"Dear Sir:—We, Hercules D. Lofty, M. D., of Mobile, Ala., Atlanta, Ga., and Paducah, Ken.; J. F. Courtney, of Columbus, Ga.; Major J. F. Shelton, of Atlanta, Ga.; Captain J. C. Carter, of Charleston, S. C.; Captain Henry A. Watson, of New Orleans, La., certify that we have accompanied you on this your last expedition to this point; the first three of us were with you on your first trip. We have witnessed, and are cognizant of the cause of your wrong, and of the efforts you have made to right it. Having remained with you throughout your stay at this point, we now cordially endorse your action throughout, and declare your family honor vindicated, and your antagonist shamed.

"We are, dear sir, your obedient servants,

"Hercules D. Lofty, M. D.,
"J. F. Courtney, M. D.,
"J. F. Shelton,
"Henry A. Watson,
"J. C. Carter."

I also take the liberty of copying two letters from Captain Porter, published also in the "Herald," as follows:

"Neil's Landing, Fla., Sept. 3, 2 p. m.

"Major J. F. Woodson.

"My Dear Sir:—You grossly injured and insulted me by your published card of 25th June. For fifty days I have persistently sought redress. You have, in every instance, evaded, while pretending to meet me.

"I now demand from you the satisfaction due between gentlemen, and require an immediate answer.

"With profound respect,

"I am your obedient servant,

"T. J. Porter."

"I certify that I saw Captain Porter hand the above note to Colonel Hercules D. Lofty.

"J. F. Shelton."

"NEIL'S LANDING, FLA., 6 P. M., 6th Sept., 1873.

"MAJOR J. F. WOODSON.

"MY DEAR SIR:—Your favor of 28th August, handed to Colonel Hercules D. Lofty, in presence of Mr. Count Bismarck and Colonel Hurd, which my friend refused to bear, on the ground that it was insulting, is unsatisfactory.

"You, sir, first insulted and then evaded me in every way. I, therefore, assume the right—which I have—to declare your card of the 25th of June to be *false* and *untrue* in *every* particular. I declare you to be a man who has slandered the dead, yet shrink from meeting one of his living relations.

"I, therefore, respectfully proclaim you to the world as Nidering! as lost to Los and honor! and dismiss you to the contempt of the world.

"With somewhat lessened respect,

"I remain, sir, your obedient servant,

"T. J. PORTER."

"I certify that Captain Porter handed the above note to Colonel Hercules D. Lofty, in my presence.

"J. F. SHELTON."

For these admirable letters to affect Major Woodson, they must have been delivered to him; but written, as they were, merely to clear the honor of Captain Porter, a delivery to Major Woodson was entirely unnecessary; but Colonel Lofty, whose grasping mind took in everything, provided against all possible technical objection, on account of the failure to deliver them to Major Woodson, by causing Captain Porter to deliver them formally to himself, in the presence of a witness. (Oh, that I could have been there to witness the impos-

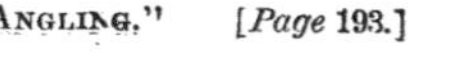

"This considerate Officer informed Colonel Lofty as to the best points for Angling." [*Page* 193.]

ing ceremony!) And, in his magnificent generosity, acting for the moment, as it were, as Major Woodson's proxy, took upon himself, spiritually, all the censure which could, by possibility, attach to Major Woodson, reminding one forcibly of that ancient ceremony, whereby one spotless, perfect animal was elected to bear the sins of an entire nation.

On reliable information, believed true, I state that the Sheriff of Jackson County kindly met Colonel Lofty and his party at Neil's Landing, and consented to receive their hospitality during their entire stay. This considerate officer informed Colonel Lofty as to the best points for angling, and courteously remained with the party while they indulged in that fascinating sport. This well-meant attention of the Sheriff made the spiritual delivery of the notes, by proxy, above-mentioned, a matter of great delicacy and eminent peril—but what is peril where honor is at stake?

The period of time necessary to wash clean the honor of Captain Porter having expired, Colonel Lofty returned to Atlanta, and aired it in the columns of the "Herald," by allowing almost all the correspondence to be printed in that paper.

CHAPTER XL.

COMMENTS OF THE PRESS.

THE correspondence between Colonel Lofty, Major Woodson, Mr. Hardy and myself, and between Captain Porter and Major Woodson, being all published, even fear of Colonel Lofty could restrain the press no longer; and I insert a few comments clipped from the journals of the day.

The stupendous advance of the American press, which, by means of its agents, interviewers, and correspondents, collects and delineates its facts equally from the distant foray, and the wild river bank, as from the crowded mart, cannot be too much admired, and the general accuracy of whose statements, in the present instance, I have no reason to question.

"SUN."

"The 'Herald' understands, that Colonel Hercules D. Lofty, M. D., intends to visit Opelika on Monday next. Gentlemen here apprehend more duelistic troubles. The several statements this man has repeated concerning our city editor were originated, and exist only, in Mr. Lofty's heated imagination."

"THE UNION AND RECORDER."

"After waiting until out of all patience, the party in Florida, it is said, picked up a stable door, and, after marking the size of their antagonist on the door, set it against a tree, and measuring off the distance sanctioned by the code, drove a ball through the centre of it. If this is true, the party in Alabama ought, in honor, to acknowledge, if he had been there, in place of the door, he would have been shot; but instead of that, he pertinaciously denies through the newspapers, that he has been killed either in person or vicariously. But this controversy has revealed a perfect prodigy in the person of Colonel or Doctor Lofty. If we knew which title he preferred, we would give it to him, for we don't wish to offend a man who has fought forty-two duels, and has been thrust through the heart, liver, lights, and midriff, as often as Jack Falstaff was through the hose and doublet. It is said, he thinks no more of killing five or six men before breakfast than he does of drinking a mint julep. That is awful! As he is the only specimen of a live Anthropophagi ever seen in this country, it would pay well if he could be carried about and exhibited. His cage should be very strong, or people will be afraid to come near enough to look at him."

"WEEKLY NEWS."

"'NIDERING,' 'LOS,' AND 'SPIRITUAL NOSE-PULLING.'—Our State exchanges are feasting over these expressions, which emanated from the recent muss between Porter, Woodson, Lofty, De Soto, *et al.*, wherein Porter, in his final denunciation of Woodson, makes use of the following: 'I, therefore, proclaim you to the world as *Nidering!* as lost to *Los* and honor!' The question now perplexing and being agitated by the Press is, where the devil did the war-horses get the words '*Los*' and '*Nidering*.'

"The 'spiritual nose-pulling' is Colonel Lofty's invention. He stated that he did not, in reality, pull the nose of the city editor of the 'Sun,' but he did do it 'spiritually.'

"The 'Enquirer' has gone to immense expense to search out the mysterious 'Los.' The editor of that paper has succeeded in furnishing us a little light on the subject:

"'*Los* is a word that we cannot fathom, and therefore it must mean something terrible. When Daniel O'Connell had his fuss with a fish woman, and demolished her by saying "She was a hypothenuse, and a parallelogram in petticoats," he could have settled her hash in an instant, by telling her she was "lost to Los." Our philological editor has scratched himself bald trying to find this word. We saw him last night diving into dictionaries and encyclopædias that rose about him as he read like a block house. He thinks the word is Modoc, and means the same as "Keno;" but this is not satisfactory, for it explains one hard word by another. Who knows the meaning of "Keno" in this land? A dispatch received per cable, an hour ago, from the celebrated philologist, Max Müller, reads as follows:

"'"LIMBURG, STATE OF NASSAU, GERMANY.
"'"September 17th, Midnight.

"'"*Los* is a Gaelic word, or rather Erse. It is now nearly obsolete, and means a man without any tail to his coat. It was once used in Ireland, when fighting was more in vogue, it being the custom of those impetuous people who were always anxious to fight anybody, to wear long coat-tails, which dragged behind them for several yards on the ground, and the person stepping on the coat-tail, challenged as it were, the coat-tailee, and the coat-tailee at once turned, and belted the coat-tailor over the head, with a complicated weapon known as a shillalah. Some of the people, under the influence of Christianity, and a dread of sore heads, abbreviated their coat-tails, so as to avoid being insulted; and thereat, the long-coat-tailmen became indignant, and called them 'Los.' But why they called them 'Los,' I am at this moment at a 'Los' to state. The 'Los' people are now legally in the majority, and men wear coat-tails for convenience, and not as the means of kicking up a rumpus.

" ' " MAX MÜLLER.

" ' " Collect $196.14."

" The 'Enquirer' also has the following:

" 'Last night a man rushed into our office, with anger in his eye, a club in his hand, and a short clay pipe in his mouth. He wore a long-tailed coat, and he announced his presence by a whoop that would make Santanta die with envy; and as he whirled his stick above his head, he screamed, "Do Oi luck loike a Los?" He struck an offensive attitude, that influenced our ready answer of "No, my friend, your coat-tail is too long." "Too the divil wid ye an' me coat-tail. The word ain't Oirish, an' if ye don't take it back, by this and by that, I'll wallop ye till yer tailor wouldn't know ye!"

" 'This incarnate and blood-thirsty fiend held out a piece of yellow paper, and ordered us to "print it at once, or prepare for a wake." "Soothe thy irate feelings, friend, thy injunctions shall be complied with," we said, in a soothing way. He left; and informed us that he would be round in the morning, and he "wanted it wurd fur wurd, and lether fur lether."

"'Here it is:

"'"COLUMBUS, GEORGY,
"'"Siptimber 18th, 1873.

"'"EDITHER INKWIRER:

"'"SUR:—In yer durty sheet, this morning, ye accuse the Oirish unjusty, an ye say what ain't so be no manner of manes, an if ye dont publish this an say so, I wouldn't give tuppince fur yer hide fur practicle purposes.—Whose Max Mule—r? I'd like to know! He's dutchman that niever sot fut on the ould sod, an if he dared to do it the insulted gintlemen of that nation would fill him as fall uf holes as a siv. He's a desaver, fur he knows in his heart, if he has any, and it's my opinion he hasn't fur he has all stummack, loike a bellus, that 'Los' ain't Oirish, but a dutch worrud, an manes 'spiled cheese.' Whin i was at Hidilburg larnin langige, for which I have a natural tashte, I got this kink. Cheese in Garminny, ye know, has to be purty bad before they called it 'spiled,' an have no use for it, and so the stheudints bear wid a man a long time before they call him 'Los,' or 'spiled cheese,' and they only do it whin a fellow won't take a dhrop of the cray-ther, and throw the rest in a man's face to git up a foight. I did this to Max Mule—r, mesilf, and begorra he wiped his face and wint out widthout saying a wurd, and thin the byes called him 'Los,' and now he takes revinge by atthribitin the wurd to my nation.

"'"Retract or die!

"'"LARRY FLAGHERTY."'"

"ALBANY NEWS."

"'NIDERING.'—It is now a matter of the utmost importance to that large and respectable class of peacemakers, who are engaged in the sensation business, and are responsible for the integrity of the code, and the quelling of perturbed spirits, to know all about this exhumed epithet.

"We have, at great labor and midnight toiling, searched the best authorities, and find that an old man by the name of Noah Webster, who was born in a little town called Hartford, in the State of Connecticut, about three miles from the centre of that village, in a small house that was covered with boards, and had a stick-and-dirt chimney, just before day, on the morning of the 16th of October, 1758—thoroughly comprehended its beauty and its uses, and fully accounted for its etymology.

"Here is what that good old man tells us about it:

"'NIDERING, *a.* (See Niding). Infamous; dastardly. "On pain of being held faithless, mansworn, and nidering." *W. Scott.*

"'NIDING, *n.* (Written also *Nithing.*) [A.-S. *Nidhing*, from *Nidth*, wickedness, malice, hatred; Dan. & Sw. *Niding;* Icel. *Nidingr.*] A despicable coward; a dastard. (*Obs.*)

"'NITHING, *n.* (See Niding.) A coward; a dastard; a poltroon. (*Obs.*)'

"There now, we have given all Uncle Noah knew about 'Nidering,' and don't want to be asked any more questions about it. John Lyde Wilson overlooked it when compiling the code."

CHAPTER XLI.

COLONEL LOFTY VISITS OPELIKA.

On the 16th of September, Colonel Lofty arrived in Opelika; his intention to do so having been first published in the "Herald." His unconquerable courage induced him to come unarmed, and almost unattended; and so reckless was he of life, that he actually walked the streets of Opelika with only one attendant, and at one time, requested even that gentleman to walk not with him, but twenty-one and one-half paces behind him.

On the morning of the 18th of September, among the letters brought me from the mail, was the following from Colonel Lofty:

"OPELIKA, ALA., September 17, 1873, 10:30 A. M.

"COLONEL G. W. HURD, *present en ville:*

"MY DEAR SIR:—Upon the 30th of August you sent me a letter, through the mail, which bore date inside, 29th of August.

"This letter, you claimed, was in reply to mine to you of 23d of August, to which you had neglected to reply. Failing to get an answer, I left Atlanta, came to Opelika, and addressed you a note, through Mr. Charley Chip, to whom you gave a verbal reply, pleading, in your usual evasive manner, that you would reply, but hadn't time then. I then sent you a second note, to which you attempted an evasive answer, which Mr. Chip refused to receive, saying to you, that he demanded a written reply to a written note.

"You then promised him that you would reply by 10 A. M. of the 30th, stating, that you preferred replying to my letter of 23d before my later ones; and, as that had been sent through the mail, you asked leave of Mr. Chip to send the reply the same way, assuring him, that, when sent, you were of opinion that I would not ask a reply to the two last.

"Mr. Chip referred the matter to me, and I consented to wait.

"At 10:30 A. M. of the next day, Mr. Chip brought me your reply.

"I am sorry, George W. Hurd, you should ever have written it—because I am sorry to cease to think you a gentleman. I had believed you one, and had treated you with courtesy accordingly.

"But, Colonel George W. Hurd, from the time you wrote that letter you were no longer a gentleman—because, sir, you had wilfully, deliberately, and with premeditation, LIED—lied, sir; not once, but many times; for, Mr. Hurd, your heart tells you that no such conversation as you report, ever passed between us; therefore you had no such memory. Oh, sir! sir! how could you degrade yourself so shamefully?

"When I had read your letter, I at once sent you a reply by Captain Carter, stating what you know well to be true—that business of greater importance prevented my replying then, and that I would reply at my convenience. You know what that business was, for you had brought me Mr. Hardy, the day before, and witnessed our interview. You were aware, I am sure, too, of the telegram he sent, after his return home, requesting me to come to Columbus. Hence, you fully understand what was meant by business of a more imperative nature.

"This note, sir, was sent to you by the hands of Captain Carter at once, and he found that you had left the city immediately upon mailing your insult to me. Captain Carter went to your office to deliver my note, found that you had left, and endorsed the fact upon the back of the note, and stated to me, that he would hunt you until he found you. There were accredited to you, besides Captain John C. Carter, also Major Shelton, and Captain Wilson. These gentlemen found you at Columbus, when they went to deliver my reply to Mr. J. T. Hardy, in General Rock's office.

"Captain Carter, as the immediate custodian of the note, asked to see you alone, as there were others present. You took him to a private room; as he entered, you drew and cocked a pistol, which you held behind you, and retreated backward behind a large table. Captain C. is a small man, unarmed. You refused the note with the pistol in your hand; but Carter told you that you must receive it, and you took it. It required no answer, yet you wrote one, stating, that as the correspondence had been commenced by mail, you proposed to continue it that way. Upon entering that room, you shut the door in the face of Captain Wilson and Major Shelton, and stood alone with Captain Carter, and drew your pistol. Oh, sir! are you not ashamed, as you remember this scene?

"Well, sir, as soon as the Porter-Woodson matter was finished, I, as I had promised, left Atlanta for

"Oh, Sir, are you not ashamed as you remember this Scene.

[*Page* 202.]

this point, *alone and unarmed.* It was my intention, if I met you on the street, to say to you, personally and privately, that you had *lied*, and dismiss the matter. I run around here all day yesterday for that purpose, and no other. I saw you but once—that was, as I returned from the 'telegraph office.' You were standing on the porch of your office. An elderly gentleman was sitting on your porch, reading. Mr. Fred. Smith was with me. I said to Mr. Smith, at once, to leave me, and not approach nearer to me than twenty-one and one-half paces. He did so, and I walked alone to the front of your office.

"As you saw me coming, and while I was yet thirty or forty yards away, you turned suddenly and went into your office; the old gentleman, too, looked at me, rose, and left the porch. (I have been told, that so soon as you got inside, you seized a double-barreled shot gun, and watched for my coming through the door.)

"Of course, I never contemplated going into your 'office.' I paused for a second, in front, then walked slowly on to the 'post-office;' waited there some three minutes, then sauntered slowly over to the hotel.

"Since that time I have been three times past your 'office,' but, save that time, have never seen you.

"Every one in this city has been a witness to the manner in which a party of your friends attempted to bully and intimidate me yesterday, by parading the streets heavily armed, and posting themselves near the door of the hotel, where I was stopping. I have been told that you were with that party. If so, you remained inside some of the doors, for I did not see you, though I saw the others, as I passed through.

"Now, Colonel Hurd, failing to see you, I mail you this reply to your extraordinary letter, and close all correspondence with you forever. There is only one way I shall ever notice you again—that is, if you should send a friend to me with a polite note, requesting me to meet you on mutual ground, your friend shall be received, and I promise to grant your wish, and restore you to the gentility you have forfeited.

"I remain here until 12 to-night, when I go to Columbus. I shall stay there twenty-four hours, and then return to Atlanta.

"I am, sir, entirely at your service,

"HERCULES D. LOFTY, M. D."

It was with great pain that I perceived, on reading this letter, that owing to one or two hasty, and doubtless unintentional, expressions, I must, under the code, return it to the distinguished writer. In taking this course, however, I could but admire those noble traits of character exhibited by the Colonel in this feeling letter. It is true that his great mind being swayed to earth, as it were, by a whirlwind of passion (caused by some malicious knave who, possessed of the garb and address of a gentleman, had insinuated himself into the Colonel's confidence, and persuaded him that my respectful letter, of the 29th, was designed to offend him), had induced him to use expressions in his last letter more usual among shoulder-hitters than among gentlemen.

Yet the general tone of his letter showed that he wrote more in grief than in anger. And the chivalrous magnanimity of the man could not, even in the moment of extreme emotion, be wrested from his heart. For it will be noted, by some with astonishment, that in the last paragraph, while under the influence of uncontrollable agitation, with reason, for the moment, driven from her throne, he believed I had lost the position of a gentleman. Yet he gallantly offered to "restore me to the gentility (he thought) I had forfeited," by a meeting which might cost his life-blood!

Natural affection may cause a mother to risk life for her babe. But nothing, save that high sense of honor implanted by the code, and exemplified so ably in Colonel Lofty, could impel a man to offer his life to restore one, who, he thought, had injured him, to the gentility he had forfeited.

While my admiration of Colonel Lofty was so greatly increased, by having it exemplified that passion, which leaves most men bereft, not only of reason, but of generosity, could only affect him so far as to cause the use of expressions not considered courteous among gentlemen, but left his generosity and magnanimity unimpaired; still, under the code, I was compelled to return his note, and I afterwards had the pain of seeing it published in the "Constitution" and "Herald," which Colonel Lofty had, I doubt not, inadvertently allowed, without a reperusal of it; and the copy which I have placed in this chapter was clipped from one of those papers.

On seeing this letter published, it, of course, became necessary for me to explain to the public (which always takes a deep interest in the honor of gentlemen) a fact which Colonel Lofty had omitted to state, and the following card was published in the "Constitution" and "Herald:"

"September 23d, 1873.

"EDITORS 'CONSTITUTION' AND 'HERALD.'

"GENTLEMEN:—Pardon my troubling you in reference to the correspondence between Colonel Lofty and myself. That gentleman has done me an injustice (unintentionally, I have no doubt), by publishing his last letter to me, and omitting to state the fact, that it was, immediately upon my receipt of it, returned to him through the mail. It was with great regret that I pursued this course, and no personal disrespect was intended to the Colonel, but, owing to the fact that his letter contained expressions (induced, doubtless, by the necessary hurry of his reply) which, by the rules of the code, had to be considered discourteous and inadmissible, I was compelled to return it, and deprive myself of the pleasure of answering. I am pleased to be able to clip a copy, which I place in my manuscript work, entitled 'Down the River,' etc.

"I remain, very respectfully,

"G. W. HURD."

CHAPTER XLII.

COLONEL LOFTY VISITS COLUMBUS.—COMMENTS OF THE PRESS.—REPORT OF THE NIGHT POLICE.

At the hour of 12 : 20 P. M., on the 18th day of September, Colonel Lofty stepped on the train at Opelika, and arrived in the city of Columbus at 3 : 30 P. M., his movements being announced through the columns of the "Herald," and other journals, as follows:

"HERALD," SEPT. 18th.

"By a special telegram, we learn that Colonel Hercules D. Lofty, M. D., will leave Opelika for Columbus, on the 12 : 20 P. M. train. It is hoped no blood will be shed in his affair with Captain De Soto.

"We learn from a friend of Colonel Lofty, that he states that he pulled, not the flesh and blood nose of Captain De Soto, but his spiritual nose, and if Mr. De Soto will admit this, Colonel Lofty will be satisfied."

"SUN," SEPT. 19th.

"H. D. Lofty came to the city on the 3 : 30 P. M. train, according to his programme, published in the 'Herald.' The object of his visit we know not, and care as little. We have simply denounced as gross falsehood, and still do so, every statement he made regarding us, which falsehoods he traveled out of his duelistic correspondence to wantonly introduce.

"We desire also to state, that the rumor that he pulled our nose in *any sense*, is as false as any statement he has made.

"De Soto, City Editor.'"

"LOFTY—DE SOTO.

"'HERALD' SPECIAL REPORT FROM COLUMBUS, Sept. 19th, 1873.

"All quiet and serene. Colonel Lofty is occasionally seen on the streets. De Soto is attending to his usual duties. Numbers gathered at the 'Sun' office this morning, as it was thought that a difficulty might occur on account of De Soto's card. The crowd dispersed in a short time. Colonel Lofty leaves to-night or in the morning. X."

"OPELIKA OBSERVER," SEPT. 19th, 1873.

"The greatest wonder of the age, Colonel Hercules Diogenes Lofty, M. D., after remaining in our city for two days, departed for Columbus on yesterday. We are happy to report that he did no material damage while here; a careful reckoning shows that none of our inhabitants have been destroyed."

Important business prevented my accompanying Colonel Lofty on this important and perilous journey, and I am only able to give meagre accounts of what occurred, ascertained from reliable gentlemen.

While on this visit to Columbus, Colonel Lofty resided at the Rankin House, Room number 10, and on the day of his arrival, at the hour of 3 : 40 P. M., accompanied by a single friend, he walked in a dignified and fearless manner, down the southern side of Perry street, the office of the "Sun" being on the northern side of the same street. At the hour of 5 : 30 he again walked in the same manner, accompanied by the same friend, down the same side of the same street; and during his entire stay in the city he continued in the same manner to walk down the same side of said street, on an average of once every three hours, rarely accompanied by more than one friend; and one of my informants reports, that in one of these walks, when Colonel Lofty had arrived at a point directly opposite the "Sun" office, and only seventy feet from it, he deliberately paused, and placed the first finger of his left hand by the side of his nose, at the same time placing the thumb of his right hand between the second and third fingers thereof, and then twisted said last-mentioned hand around several times. This last information may possibly be incorrect, as my informant states the remarkable circumstance to have occurred at 9 : 20 P. M., and that the street at that point was indifferently lighted.

Be that as it may, all who had any desire to be so, were convinced that Colonel Lofty knew not the feeling of fear, and was prepared for any emergency which might arise.

At 1 A. M. of the 20th, an incident occurred, of which I am forced to give only the version of the police, not having been present myself, and not having seen Colonel Lofty since, to get the true state of facts.

The report of two policemen was as follows:

Policeman No. 1. At 1 A. M. 23d September, saw a tall gentleman, in Tenth Ward, bowing to a lamp-post several times; considering the action singular, continued to notice him, and called the attention of Pat O'Connor. As we watched, at 1:03 A. M., tall gentleman went forward to the lamp-post and put both his arms around it. Pat O'Connor then went up to tall gentleman and asked him his name. Tall gentleman straightened himself and bowed, first to me, and then to Pat, and said his name was Hercules Diogenes Lofty, M. D., and that he resided at the Rankin House, Room No. 10, and then he requested Pat and myself to search him and see if he had any arms, which we did, and found none. He then asked us to let the people of Columbus know, early next morning, that Hercules Diogenes Lofty, M. D., was alone and unarmed, so that they might resume their ordinary occupations without fear, and begged us to state further to the people, that he would not interfere with any of them if they attended quietly to their own business and did not offend him in any way. He then asked Pat and myself to take a drink with him, which we did, going for that purpose to the *Sans Souci*. And then we walked with the tall gentleman to the Rankin House, Room No. 10, and he laid down with his boots on, stating that he considered it true courtesy not to pull his boots off so early, for that, if a friend called and asked him out to take a drink, it would be impolite to keep him waiting, while he was pulling his boots on.

Report of Policeman No. 2, was to the effect that the report of No. 1 was true in each detail, but, he added, "that the tall gintleman was the cliverest and the perlitist gintleman he had iver seen this side of the Ould Country."

And thus we see, even by the meagre and dry report

'He then Requested Pat and Myself to Search Him and See if he had any Arms."

[*Page* 210.]

of the night police, the thoughtful and kind consideration of this great man, exemplified in his great care for the people, and his desire to keep them peaceful and happy, and free from alarm and terror. His own greatness and notoriety he could not avoid, but to the extent of his ability he allayed the fears of the people.

At 11 A. M. of the 20th, Mr. Hardy encountered Colonel Lofty upon the sidewalk of Broad street, as the latter emerged from the Rankin House, and accosted him thus: "Colonel Lofty, I think I understood you to say that my brother, Colonel O. S. Hardy, was an intimate friend of yours."

Lofty. My dear Colonel Hardy (bow), you certainly understood me correctly; I have no dearer friend than your brother, and he has a higher opinion of me than almost any man I know; he would do anything for me; he would go to the end of the world to serve me. I can safely refer you to him for my character, if you have the slightest doubt upon that subject. And, allow me to say, that your brother is a man whom any one might well be proud to be able to refer to for his character and standing, for I do not know of a more perfect gentleman or a more honorable man.

Hardy. I have this morning received a letter from my brother, and as it refers to you, I was on my way to your room to show it to you, when I met you just now. It is but proper, however, before I show you his letter, to state to you, that as my brother will not be here for some weeks, I, in handing you his letter, assume fully the responsibility for all he writes, or, if you prefer seeing him, in person, I will dispatch him to come on at once. Here is my brother's letter (handing Colonel Lofty the letter).

Lofty. It is with great pleasure that I read anything to which your brother's signature is affixed. With your permission I will do myself the honor of reading this letter at once; and he read it as follows:

"NEW YORK, September 17, 1873.

"DEAR BROTHER:—Your favor received, and contents noted. I hasten to reply to that portion inquiring about 'Colonel Hercules D. Lofty, M. D.'

"You say the Colonel referred you to me, as 'being an *intimate* friend.' Unfortunately (if the Colonel is the same Hercules D. Lofty I knew in Mobile), I have known him for about four or five years, and know him to be a most consummate dead-beat, and a coward. You cannot have any correspondence or intercourse with him other than to use a horsewhip on him, should he insult you. Be kind enough to hand him this, as he refers you to me for his character; and say to him, I will be South about the 10th of October.

"The hotel-keepers of Mobile can give you further information regarding the Colonel—'so called.'

"Yours truly,

"O. S. HARDY."

During the reading of this letter Mr. Hardy watched the face of Colonel Lofty with intense interest, evidently expecting an attack upon himself, at, or before, the reading of it had been completed. What, then, was his surprise, at seeing Colonel Lofty, as soon as he had finished reading the note, throw himself back, convulsed with laughter, which continued several minutes. After two or three efforts, and free use of a pocket handkerchief, Colonel Lofty so far recovered himself as to be able to speak. He then said, "Colonel, I hope you will excuse my laughter. I assure you that no offense was intended by it; but that letter—(and here he was interrupted by another irresistible fit of laughter). Your brother, sir, is one of the most gifted men I ever saw; his social qualities are unsurpassed; he is the greatest humorist I ever met; and, when he wrote that letter, he was in one of his happiest veins. I would freely give a year of my life to have been with him at that time."

Colonel Lofty then invited Mr. Hardy to drink with him.

At 10:40 P. M., of the 20th, Colonel Lofty quietly departed from the city of Columbus, *en route* for Atlanta, and it was after his arrival in that city that his letter to me of the 17th of September, and my card hereinbefore set out, were published.

On the morning of the 21st, the following appeared in the "Sun."

"ALL SERENE.

"This is the holy Sabbath morning, and we are glad that we can report all quiet along the Chattahoochee, from Atlanta to Neil's Landing. 'Grim-visaged war doth smooth his wrinkled front,' and those who were lately in lively expectation of an opening tragedy are now laughing at something else. We feel sure that the effect of the late excitement will be a wholesome one. It will make people reflect on the folly of stirring up personal quarrels, and a resort to other than peaceable means for the settlement of differences not demanding the shedding of blood. Much money has doubtless been spent—much time lost—much anxiety and excitement occasioned—and now things are in *statu quo.* Let us rejoice, that it has the appearance of a peaceable situation at last, and that the temple of Janus will be closed during a long reign of the 'piping times of peace.'"

CHAPTER XLIII.

CORRESPONDENCE BETWEEN COLONEL LOFTY AND COLONEL HURD.

On the morning of the 28th of September, 1873, I observed published in the columns of the "Constitution" and "Herald," the letter of Colonel Lofty to myself of 17th instant.

The duty of calling Colonel Lofty to account seemed now to devolve upon me, and imitating his noble example, I did my duty.

First, I sought my friend, Colonel Jasper P. Bartow, and after placing my honor in his hands, the following correspondence ensued:

"Opelika, Ala., September 29th, 1873.
"R. R. Depot, 1:20 A. M.

"Colonel Hercules D. Lofty.

"My Dear Sir:—While honor prevents my answering your favor of 17th instant, yet self-respect demands that I should ask an explanation of a part of that letter, inasmuch as it has now been published. Before doing so, however, it is my duty, and I perform it with pleasure, to explain to you that portion of my letter of 29th August, which gave you so much pain. Although your letter does not distinctly specify the point of which you complain, yet, through the kindness of our mutual friend, Colonel J. W. Houser, I am informed, that my statement of only forty-two duels in which you had been engaged, while the correct number was much greater, very naturally gave you offence, which your delicacy, in writing to me, prevented your mentioning particularly. Now, while I must say, that my recollection of the number which you stated to me in the 3:30 conversation, is still the same, yet I will add, cheerfully, that I have heard you, both before and since that time, mention a much larger number. And Dr. Jones, who is the soul of honor, informs me, that you stated to him the number of duels in which you had been engaged, to be *fifty-seven.* Now, my dear Colonel, having explained, as far as I am able, the point of difference between us, which gave rise to your favor of 17th inst., I hope you will pardon my respectfully asking of you an explanation of a part of that letter.

"I had at one time intended to ask an explanation of you of those expressions in that letter, which were disrespectful in terms, but a careful examination of the code and precedents, shows me that I cannot do so. In the first place, it being a settled maxim, that no gentleman could *intentionally* write to another gentleman in such disrespectful terms it follows that I could not presume that you, being undoubtedly a gentleman, could *intentionally* have written those expressions. And if you used them unintentionally, I do not see how I could insist upon your meeting me for a mere *lapsus pennæ*, and to require you to explain that it was unintentional on your part, would be a mere waste of time; for if you could, by possibility, violate the presumption that it was unintentional, then you would prove yourself unworthy of my recognition, which would be *reduc-*

tio ad absurdum. In other words, if you, in a letter to me, deliberately and intentionally state that I have '*lied*,' the fact that you do so write your letter, proves you not to be a gentleman, and hence I could not ask an explanation of, or meet you under any circumstances. I am, therefore, bound to presume, either that you never wrote such a letter, or that such expressions therein, as are disrespectful in terms, were *unintentional.*

"The usual presumption indulged in such cases, is, I am informed, that the writer of the letter did not write such a letter at all, and hence the custom among gentlemen arose, of returning such letters to the persons from whom they purport to come; that person, being presumed at once to see that it was a base forgery, is presumed to treat the whole matter with silent contempt, unless he finds that he did intentionally write the letter.

"But the matter which has now arisen between you and myself, is not in the usual course. Here a remarkable fact has transpired, to wit, the publication of your letter of the 17th, after it had been returned to you, without first sending a note to me to require an explanation of my returning it.

"In this most unprecedented case, then, I must presume that your letter of the 17th was not a forgery, and I must also presume, that the expressions referred to were unintentional.

"The point, however, on which I respectfully ask an explanation of you, is of much graver import. Your letter admits that you were in Opelika on the 16th of September, and had passed by my office (the precise hour not given); that you had seen me on the porch of my office, and that you paused a moment in front of my door, and then passed on, without entering. And you say, that you never even contemplated entering my office.

"I assure you, sir, that this action on your part has caused me great grief, and I am compelled to ask you to explain why you should pass my office, knowing me to be within, without calling. The excuse which you make in your letter, I am compelled to say, does not satisfy me. Ordinary men might be supposed to be afraid of a double-barreled gun leveled at them, but for you, Colonel Lofty, to make such a paltry excuse as that to me! Oh, sir! how could you attempt it, after explaining to me the thousands of deadly perils you had encountered; after I had seen you; after I had known you!

"I must, therefore, ask you to be kind enough to explain to me your most astonishing and unaccountable action, in not calling to see me when you passed my office.

"This letter will be handed you by my friend, Colonel Jasper P. Bartow, to whom I beg to introduce you, and who will be the bearer of your reply to me.

"I remain, dear Colonel, with profound respect,

"Your obedient servant,

"George W. Hurd."

"P. S.—As an excuse for the delay of thirteen days, in asking an explanation of your most singular conduct in passing my office without calling, I have only to say, that the astounding and unprecedented nature of the offence you thereby gave me, and the pain and grief thereby inflicted, were so great, that I could not recover sufficiently therefrom to write you before this A. M.

And, in addition, I think that my pain at your action can only be considered as commencing from the time of the publication of your letter; before that time, your letter, having been returned to you, could not be considered as paining me. Colonel Bartow agrees with me on this point; but another question here arises: you caused this letter to be published on the 25th inst., and I did not see the paper containing it until the 28th. Now, the question is, did my 'pain and grief' commence on the 25th, or on the 28th. My dear Colonel, permit me to say, that I do not see, under all the circumstances, how you can claim that I was 'pained or grieved' before the 28th inst.; and this being the 29th, it follows that I have lost no time asking an explanation.

"I again sign myself, with profound respect,

"Your most obedient servant,

"GEORGE W. HURD."

"ATLANTA, GA., September 30th, 1873.
"National Hotel, Room 22, 4:10 P. M.

"COLONEL GEORGE W. HURD.

"MY DEAR SIR:—Your astonishing letter of 1:40 A. M., of 29th inst., by the hands of Colonel Jasper P. Bartow, is this moment received; and while I do myself the honor to agree with you in considering your excuse for not making an earlier demand on me as sufficient, yet, sir, I ask, as a personal favor to myself, and for my personal sake, that you allow me ten days in which to answer your most remarkable letter, hoping within that time to find some excuse satisfactory to you for my not calling on you; and should no sufficient excuse occur to my mind, then, with not more pleasure and alacrity would a lover spring to the arms of his mistress, upon their bridal night, than will I to the neighborhood of the field of honor, where we can proceed with our correspondence.

"I am, dear Colonel, very respectfully,

"Your obedient servant,

"HERCULES D. LOFTY, M. D."

This pleasant letter was handed me by Colonel Bartow, at 1:50 A. M. of 1st of October, and with earnest solicitude did we consider the momentous questions, as to whether I should allow Colonel Lofty ten days time to answer, and as to whether I could be supposed to survive so long a delay, after so singular and unprecedented an offence, as that of which I had complained. After great deliberation, we concluded to allow the time, and I wrote to Colonel Lofty as follows:

"OPELIKA, ALA., October 1st, 1873.
"At Office, 3:10 P. M.

"COLONEL HERCULES D. LOFTY.

MY DEAR SIR:—I have just had the honor of reading your polite note of 30th of September, and I assure you that it gives me great pleasure to comply with your very reasonable request. This note will be handed you by my friend, Colonel Jasper P. Bartow, who will bring me your reply at such time as may suit your perfect convenience.

"I remain, Colonel, with profound respect,

"Your most obedient servant,

"G. W. HURD."

On the tenth day of October at 1:45 P. M., I received by the hands of my friend Colonel Bartow, the following letter from Colonel Lofty:

'ATLANTA, GA., October 9, 1873.
"NATIONAL HOTEL, 3:20 P. M.

"COLONEL GEORGE W. HURD.

"MY DEAR SIR:—In reply to your courteous letter of the 29th of September, I do myself the honor of saying, that the statement of our distinguished friend, Doctor Jones—of my having been engaged in FIFTY-SEVEN affairs of honor—is correct; of course, neither the affair between Captain Porter and Major Woodson, or between myself and Colonel Strong, Major De Soto, Mr. Hardy, Major Woodson, or yourself, were included in that number. It would have been dishonorable in me to have counted them, as they were not at that time ended, some of them not commenced, and I frequently omit to count slight affairs, which do not result in bloodshed. Now, as you agree with Doctor Jones, I must consider your apology on that point as sufficient. I will say, further, that you are entirely correct in supposing that the discourteous words used in my letter to you were entirely accidental; and now, I will address myself to the important question upon which you ask an explanation, which I will be so candid as to say is one which perplexes me greatly. I have never been engaged in but one affair in which this point was raised, and in that case the presenting a pistol, cocked and loaded, at the head of a visitor, was considered a sufficient excuse for not calling. But, sir, that man was not Hercules D. Lofty. Neither a pistol nor a gun would, for one moment, deter me from visiting a friend, or seeking an interview with an enemy; therefore, I must, being a candid man, state to you the true reason why I did not do myself the honor of calling:

"While at the telegraph office, I was told that a new

bar-room, called the 'Lyott,' had been opened near the post-office, in Opelika, in which the very best whiskey was sold, and I was hasting there to try the whiskey, and paused for a moment in front of your door, with a view to inviting you to do me the honor of drinking with me, when, reflecting that you did not drink whiskey, and not knowing about the wine at the 'Lyott,' I concluded not to ask you to drink until I had made some inquiry on that point. And, besides, I was at the moment somewhat perplexed by a point of honor, which was, whether it would not be more proper for you to invite me to drink first, as I was a visitor to your city, and I postponed calling, that I might reflect on this most intricate and perplexing question.

"I hope, my dear sir, that this full and sufficient excuse will be satisfactory to you. If it is not, I can only say, that I humbly await your pleasure.

"This note will be borne by my friend, Captain J. C. Carter, who is authorized to act for me, fully, in this matter.

"I remain, my dear Colonel,
"With profound respect,
"Your most obedient servant,
"HERCULES D. LOFTY, M. D."

It is needless to say that this sublime letter gave infinite satisfaction, both to myself and to my friend, Colonel Jasper P. Bartow, who was, however, of opinion that Colonel Lofty should have called on me on the 16th, and that, thereupon, I must necessarily have asked him to drink, and, thereafter, Colonel Lofty could have insisted on my accompanying him to the Lyott Saloon.

My reply was as follows:

"OPELIKA, ALA., October 10th, 1873.
"At Office, 2 P. M.

"COLONEL HERCULES D. LOFTY.

"DEAR SIR:—I have just had the pleasure of reading your favor of the 9th October, and have only to say, that your explanation is satisfactory in every particular, and I can only wonder at my obtuseness in not at once surmising the reason of your action.

"This note will be conveyed to your friend, Captain Carter, by my friend, Colonel Jasper P. Bartow.

"I hope you will allow me to assume the honor of signing myself, with most profound respect,

"Your obedient servant, till death,

"GEORGE W. HURD."

CHAPTER XLIV.

COLONEL LOFTY PROPOSES A PARTNERSHIP.

It is with regret that I omit from this volume an account of the progress and termination of the affair of honor between Colonel Lofty and Major Woodson, originating from the latter's remark about "poisoned liquor;" but inasmuch as nothing further has, up to this time, actually occurred, I hope that excuse will be received by my readers as sufficient for my omission. Rather than mention one fact in this history before it occurred, I would wait, and, if necessary, publish another volume.

It is almost unnecessary for me to state, that Colonel Lofty and myself, having adjusted all our differences, were impressed with a very high opinion of each other's character, courage, and courteous deportment. But to the end that no cloud of doubt may rest upon this point, I copy here a letter recently received by me from that distinguished gentleman, and my reply:

"MOBILE, ALA., 8 : 40 P. M., December 1, 1873.

"COLONEL GEORGE W. HURD, *present en ville.*

"MY DEAR COLONEL:—Since the termination of our last most delightful correspondence, you have been rarely absent from my mind. I think of you night and day.

"You will pardon me, I hope, for saying that there is but one drawback to your being now the most polished duelist on the globe. You well know to what I refer; it is to your principles, or rather prejudices, on the subject of drinking whiskey. This I consider your only weak point, and has, I candidly admit, caused me to hesitate about making you a proposition of vast importance to ourselves and to the world at large.

"But, upon mature reflection, I have arrived at the conclusion that no other man is so competent to take the position I wish you to occupy, as yourself.

"I therefore make this proposition to you: That you and myself enter into a partnership, for the purpose of advancing the noble profession of dueling.

"You are well aware that many duels are not commenced, simply and alone because the party aggrieved is unable, in these degenerate days, to procure a second.

"Now, I propose to remedy this great and increasing evil, by publishing the inclosed card. When that is done, no gentleman who is aggrieved can have any excuse for not redressing his grievance under the Code of Honor.

"While my only object in forming this partnership with you is for the good of the public, yet most decided financial advantages will necessarily accrue to ourselves, as I will here proceed to explain, * * * and exemplify by the light of my past experience * * * *

(This portion of Colonel Lofty's letter being confidential, I omit the three pages thereof relating to the subject of finance. On the fifth page, his letter continues as follows:)

"Now, my dear Colonel Hurd, in order to carry out successfully this stupendous design, which I have done you and myself the honor to conceive, it will be necessary for us to acquire as complete a mastery over the codes of honor of all nations as we have over those of America, England, and Ireland. I am now engaged in mastering the Code of Honor of Russia. I inclose you in this letter the French Code, which I know you will appreciate highly.

"And now, my dear Colonel, while anxiously awaiting your reply,

"I have the honor to remain,
"With profound respect,
"Your most obedient servant,
"HERCULES D. LOFTY, M. D."

The French Code which Colonel Lofty inclosed was as follows:

THE BRANTÔME CODE.

"*Rule* 1. On no account whatever let an infidel be brought out as a second or a witness; it is not proper that an unbeliever should witness the shedding of Christian blood, which would delight him; and it is moreover abominable that such a wretch should be allowed such an honorable pastime.

"*Rule* 2. The combatants must be carefully examined and felt, to ascertain that they have no particular drugs, witchcraft, or charms about them. It is allowed to wear on such occasions some relics of Our Lady of Loretto, and other holy objects; yet it is not clearly decided what is to be done when both parties have not these relics, as no advantage should be allowed to one combatant more than to another.

"*Rule* 3. It is idle to dwell upon courtesies: the man who steps into the field must have made up his mind to conquer or die, but above all things never to surrender; for the conqueror may treat the vanquished as he thinks proper—drag him round the ground, hang him, burn him, keep him a prisoner; in short do with him whatever he pleases.

"*Rule* 4. Every gallant Knight must maintain the honor of ladies, whether they may have forfeited it or not,—if it can be said that a *gentille dame* can have forfeited her honor by kindness to her servant and her lover.

"*Rule* 5. A soldier may fight his captain, provided he has been two years upon actual service and quits his company.*

"*Rule* 6. If a father accuses a son of any crime that may tend to dishonor him, the son may demand satisfaction of his father, since he has done him more injury by dishonoring him, than he had bestowed advantage by giving him life.

"*Rule* 7. That all challenges from a *roturier*, a mere citizen, or a man in business, must be considered as null and void.

"*Rule* 8. You can refuse to fight a bastard; it is, therefore, strongly recommended to all noblemen to legitimatize their sons, that they may be rendered worthy of the honor of Knighthood and of dueling."

* Notwithstanding the high authority of Brantôme, this is a questionable point. La Bérandière, Basnage, and Alciat, have discussed the point very minutely. The last author came to the conclusion, that such a meeting could only be tolerated when both parties were off duty—*post functionem secus.*

The card which Colonel Lofty enclosed was as follows:

"NOTICE.—The undersigned offer to the gentlemen of the world their services as seconds, in any affair of honor which may hereafter arise in any civilized country. One of us proposes to act for the challenger, and the other for the challenged. We are actuated, in making this offer to the public, not by mercenary motives, but solely for the good of the present and future generations; being satisfied that we can conduct almost any affair to a satisfactory conclusion, and embellish it with all those courtesies so necessary in such matters. Our services can only be obtained by gentlemen, as we both have an utter and unspeakable abhorrence of anything shoddy.

"Should either of the parties whom we may represent, prefer not having an actual meeting, for any reason except fear, we will adopt the quarrel, by such means as will effectually preserve the honor of both principals, and fight it out between ourselves, to a fatal conclusion, unless the matter should happen to be settled between us, amicably and honorably, by correspondence.

"While each of us shrinks from notoriety, yet, in such remarkable cases as we may find that it is necessary to preserve the honor of our principals, we will allow the correspondence to be published.

"We absolutely require those who may obtain our services, to preserve that secrecy so necessary in conducting such affairs.

"Should we find it necessary, in conducting any affair, to repair to Central Africa, or to the polar regions, we will respectfully suggest to our principals the propriety of insuring our lives, for the benefit of our helpless families.

"Humbly awaiting the pleasure of all gentlemen who

may need our services, we subscribe our names, with profound respect,

"Their most obedient servants,

"HERCULES D. LOFTY, M. D.,
"Mobile, Ala.,
"Atlanta, Ga.,
"Paducah, Ky.

"GEORGE W. HURD,
"Opelika, Ala.

"P. S.—Inasmuch as we do not desire notoriety, only those respectable journals, which are conducted solely for the public good, and are not actuated merely by a desire for private gain, have permission to publish this card—sending their bills therefor to the principals in the first affair we may do ourselves the honor to conduct.

"HERCULES D. LOFTY, M. D.,
"G. W. HURD."

After several hours of deep thought and consideration, I replied to this captivating letter as follows:

"MOBILE, ALA., 10 P. M., December 2d, 1873.

"COLONEL HERCULES D. LOFTY.

"MY DEAR SIR:—Your most remarkable letter, of 1st instant, reached me at 9 P. M., of that day.

"Now, after thirteen hours consideration, I am unable to find words to express the proud satisfaction and honor I felt at being the recipient of such a letter from such a gentleman as yourself. I am astonished at the stupendous nature and scope of the enterprise you propose. No intellect, save yours, could have conceived of such a proposition. No heart, save yours, would have dared to undertake it.

"While I feel incompetent to fill the position to which you propose to assign me, yet the honor you confer on me, by offering it, is so great, and the benefit to the public so surprising, that I scarcely know how gracefully to decline your noble offer. But I must decline; not altogether on account of my incompetency (for a prolonged intercourse with yourself would, doubtless, remove that objection), but my professional engagements are such, at present, as make it impossible for me to enter into the partnership you propose.

"Should you, however, in the future be engaged in any such remarkable affairs of honor as might admit of being recorded for the benefit of the present and future generations, it will afford me much pleasure to record them for you, and to see that the public have a correct version thereof.

"It was with great pleasure that I read the French Code, by Brantôme, which you did me the kindness to inclose in your last; it is short, but very comprehensive. I was much surprised this morning, to hear a French gentleman, to whom I was speaking of it, in terms of praise, say that it was scarcely recognized in France now, and that a more recent code had taken its place. This gentleman was kind enough to lend me the code to which he referred, which I inclose to you, hoping for your opinion on this interesting subject.*

"I now take the liberty of signing myself, with greatly enhanced respect and esteem,

"Your most humble and obedient servant,

"G. W. Hurd."

---

* For French Code, see Appendix.

POSTSCRIPT.

WHY may not a book have a "postscript" as well as a letter? Take a case like mine in writing this book: after the type is set, a *fact* occurs relating to the hero; is it not admissible to stop the printers and induce them to add a short postscript? Now, in any work of fiction, a postscript might be considered inadmissible, for if the writer is at liberty to invent his facts, of course there is nothing easier than to have all the dates and facts arranged before the work reaches the printer, cause the hero to walk in marble halls, and sleep on beds of eider-down, if not throughout the book, at least in the concluding chapter; and a most lovely and virtuous heroine may be invented to soften the jagged outlines of your tale.

But note the contrast when you are confined to facts alone. Only one lady is herein even referred to, and she remained but a moment on the stage, and might scarcely have been noticed had not the eagle glance of Colonel Lofty observed her beauteous form, and singled her out as he made his "*dashing descent*."

The facts which I add this postscript to narrate, occur at an inconvenient time, and except that some great principles and important law questions are involved, might be omitted. They are stated quite accurately in the *Herald*, and other journals, copies of which reached me this (Saturday) morning.

I only give an outline of the facts. One of these journals says:

"The very small distance from the sublime (?) to the ridiculous, so frequently alluded to by public speakers and writers, received a practical illustration in Atlanta on Wednesday last.

"The celebrated Colonel (?), alias Doctor (?), who is gifted with an extraordinary memory—and once had a fool for a second—it seems lodged and boarded for a considerable length of time at the National Hotel in that city, and drank at the bar of said hotel divers kinds and varieties of liquors, principally, however, of the beverage known by the vulgar name of whiskey, and in addition to the drinks taken and consumed by the Colonel (?) in his own proper person, divers and sundry other persons did drink at said bar, at and upon and by the express invitation of the said Colonel, the barkeeper understanding that the Colonel did thereby *impliedly* become responsible for said drinks. It appears that nearly two months ago, the Colonel, being annoyed by the pertinacious applications for money made upon him by the agents, proprietors, and managers of said hotel, quietly left it after supper one night, or before breakfast next morning—there seems to have been some conflict as to the exact time.* That he left in his apartment a quantity of baggage consisting of two large dry-goods boxes, supposed to contain his wearing apparel.

"Now, the proprietor of said hotel failing to receive a reply to any of the numerous letters addressed by him to the Colonel, did, after his departure on last Wednesday morning, cause and procure a writ of attachment to be placed in the hands of the sheriff and levied upon the baggage aforesaid, upon which the officer made the following return:

"'ATLANTA, GA., Feb. 12, 1874.

"'Levied the within attachment on two dry-goods boxes, measuring each 2ft. × 4ft. × 6ft., marked H. D. L., M.D., and containing three two-gallon demijohns, four one-gallon jugs, thirteen quart flasks, seventy-three quart bottles, all empty; one pair of dueling pistols in a case. Pistols

* I do not see that in this instance time is material.

and case supposed to be worth $17.50, balance of plunder above specified worth $5.50, pointed out to me as the property of Colonel Hercules D. Lofty, M. D. No other property to be found in my county on which to levy this attachment.

"'JOHN H. HOPKINS,
"'*Sheriff.*'

"It is stated on most reliable information that the pistols mentioned in this levy were the identical pistols used by Colonel Hercules D. Lofty, M. D., on both the expeditions which he made to Florida in the Porter-Woodson affair of honor.

"These facts were related by one of the attorneys in the cause to a knot of lawyers in the Solicitor General's office yesterday, when a very distinguished lawyer remarked that he thought in this case dueling pistols ought to be exempt from levy and sale, they being the 'implements of Colonel Lofty's trade.'"

Notwithstanding the opinion thus publicly expressed of the eminent lawyer referred to in the above copied article, it is generally understood that the attorneys of the plaintiff in attachment will contend that the pistols are not exempt, and admitting the facts that they are the implements of Colonel Lofty's trade, and that the law of Georgia exempts the implements of a man's trade from levy and sale, yet they hope by some legal quibble or technicality to avoid the logical force of these propositions. Can they do it? Will the judiciary of Georgia permit it? Be their decision what it may, certain it is that Colonel Lofty has not been treated in this instance with that courtesy inculcated by the code. Colonel Lofty would, I am certain, had he been requested in a polite manner, have presented to the proprietor of the National all the bottles, jugs, flasks, and demijohns (they being empty) seized by the sheriff, and his generosity would doubtless have led him to add the two dry-goods boxes, making an attachment entirely unnecessary.

And there can be no doubt that the leaving of the pistols among these empty bottles, etc., was an oversight on the part of Colonel Lofty, occasioned doubtless by the hurry of his departure from Atlanta. Now, is it fair? is it just? is it in accordance with the code of honor, that advantage should be taken of the mere oversight of the Colonel, and that his pistols should be thus seized by the minions of the law?

It is with regret that I close this book without answering any of the perplexing questions which have occurred to my mind since being informed of the facts above stated.

APPENDIX.

THE AMERICAN CODE.

CODE OF HONOR;

OR,

RULES FOR THE GOVERNMENT OF PRINCIPALS AND SECONDS IN DUELING.

BY JOHN LYDE WILSON.

TO THE PUBLIC.

THE man who adds in any way to the sum of human happiness is strictly in the discharge of a moral duty. When Howard visited the victims of crime and licentiousness, to reform their habits and ameliorate their condition, the question was never asked whether he had been guilty of like excesses or not. The only question the philanthropist would propound should be: Has the deed been done in the true spirit of Christian benevolence?

Those who know me can well attest the motive which has caused the publication of the following sheets, to which they for a long time urged me in vain. Those who do not know me have no right to impute a wrong motive; and if they do, I had rather be the object than the authors of condemnation.

To publish a CODE OF HONOR, to govern in cases of individual combat, might seem to imply that the publisher was an advocate of dueling, and wished to introduce it as the proper mode of deciding all personal difficulties and misunderstandings. Such implication would do me great injustice.

But if the question were directly put to me whether there are not cases where duels are right and proper, I would unhesitatingly answer: There are. If an oppressed nation has a right to appeal to arms in defence of its liberty and the happiness of its people, there can be no argument used in support of such appeal which will not apply with equal force to individuals. How many cases are there that might be enumerated where there is no tribunal to do justice to an oppressed and deeply-wronged individual? If he be subjected to a tame submission to insult and disgrace, where no power can shield him from its effects, then, indeed, it would seem that the first law of nature, self-preservation, points out the only remedy for his wrongs.

The history of all animated nature exhibits a determined resistance to encroachments upon natural rights—nay, I might add, inanimate nature; for it also exhibits a continual warfare for supremacy. Plants of the same kind, as well as trees, do not stop their vigorous growth because they overshadow their kind, but, on the contrary, flourish with greater vigor as the more weak and delicate decline and die. Those of different species are at perpetual warfare.

The sweetest rose-tree will sicken and waste away on the near approach of the noxious bramble, and the most promising fields of wheat yield a miserable harvest if choked up with tares and thistles. The elements themselves war together, and the angels of heaven have met in fierce encounter. The principle of self-preservation is co-extensive with creation, and when by education we make character and moral worth a part of ourselves, we guard our possessions with more watchful zeal than life itself, and would go farther for their protection. When one finds himself avoided in society, his friends shunning his approach, his substance wasting, his wife and children in want around him, and traces all his misfortunes and misery to the slanderous tongue of the calumniator, who, by secret whisper or artful innuendo, had sapped and undermined his reputation, he must be more or less than man to submit in silence.

The indiscriminate and frequent appeal to arms, to settle trivial disputes and misunderstandings, cannot be too severely censured and deprecated. I am no advocate for such dueling. But in cases where the laws of the country give no redress for injuries received, where public opinion not only authorizes but enjoins resistance, it is needless and a waste of time to denounce the practice. It will be persisted in as long as a manly independence and a lofty personal pride in all that dignifies and ennobles the human character shall continue to exist. If a man be smote on one cheek in public, and he turns the other which is also smitten; and he offers no resistance, but blesses him that so despitefully uses him, I am aware he is in the exercise of great Christian forbearance, highly recommended and enjoined by many very good men, but utterly repugnant to those feelings which nature and education have implanted in the human character.

If it was possible to enact laws so severe and impossible to be evaded, as to enforce such a rule of behavior, all that is honorable in the community would quit the country and inhabit the wilderness with the Indians. If such a course of conduct was infused by education into the minds of our youth, and it became praiseworthy and honorable to a man to submit to insult and indignity, then, indeed, the forbearance might be borne without disgrace.

Those, therefore, who condemn all who do not denounce dueling in every case, should establish schools where a passive submission to force would be the exercise of a commendable virtue. I have not the least doubt if, I had been educated in such a school, and lived in such a society, I would have proved a very good member of it. But I very much doubt, if a seminary of learning was established where this Christian forbearance was inculcated and enforced, whether there would be many scholars.

I would not wish to be understood to say that I do not desire to see dueling cease to exist, entirely, in society. But my plan for doing it away is essentially different from the one which teaches a passive forbearance to insult and indignity. I would inculcate in the rising generation a spirit of lofty independence. I would have them taught that nothing was more derogatory to the honor of a gentleman than to wound the feelings of any one, however humble. That, if wrong be done to another, it was more an act of heroism and bravery to repair the injury, than to persist in error, and enter into mortal combat with the injured party. That this would be an aggravation of that which was already odious, and would put him without the pale of all decent society and honorable men.

I would strongly inculcate the propriety of being tender of the feelings of those around him. I would teach immutable integrity, and uniform urbanity of manners. Scrupulously to guard individual honor, by a high personal self-respect and the practice of every commendable virtue. Once let such a system of education be universal, and we should seldom hear, if ever, of any more dueling.

The severest penal enactments cannot restrain the practice of dueling, and their extreme severity in this State the more effectually shields the offender. The teaching and preaching of our eloquent clergy may do some service, but is wholly inadequate to suppress it. Under these circumstances the following rules are given to the public, and if I can save the life of one useful member of society, I will be compensated. I have restored to the bosom of many, their sons, by my timely interference, who are ignorant of the misery I have averted from them. I believe that nine duels out of ten, if not ninety-nine out of a hundred, originate in the want of experience in the seconds. A book of authority, to which they can refer in matters where they are uninformed, will therefore be a *desideratum*. How far this code will be that book, the public must decide.

CHAPTER I.

THE PERSON INSULTED, BEFORE CHALLENGE SENT.

1. WHENEVER you believe you are insulted, if the insult be in public, and by words or behavior, never resent it there, if you have self-command enough to avoid noticing it. If resented there, you offer an indignity to the company, which you should not.

2. If the insult be by blows, or any personal indignity, it may be resented at the moment, for the insult to the company did not originate with you. But although resented at the moment, yet you are bound still to have satisfaction, and must, therefore, make the demand.

3. When you believe yourself aggrieved, be silent on the subject, speak to no one about the matter, and see your friend, who is to act for you, as soon as possible.

4. Never send a challenge in the first instance, for that precludes all negotiation. Let your note be in the language of a gentleman, and let the subject-matter of complaint be truly and fairly set forth, cautiously avoiding attributing to the adverse party any improper motive.

5. When your second is in full possession of the facts,

leave the whole matter to his judgment, and avoid any consultation with him, unless he seeks it. He has the custody of your honor, and by obeying him you cannot be compromitted.

6. Let the time of demand upon your adversary, after the insult, be as short as possible, for he has the right to double that time in replying to you, unless you give some good reason for your delay. Each party is entitled to reasonable time to make the necessary domestic arrangements, by will or otherwise, before fighting.

7. To written communication you are entitled to a written reply, and it is the business of your friend to require it.

SECOND'S DUTY BEFORE CHALLENGE SENT.

1. Whenever you are applied to by a friend to act as his second, before you agree to do so, state distinctly to your principal that you will be governed only by your own judgment, that he will not be consulted after you are in full possession of the facts, unless it becomes necessary to make or accept the *amende* honorable, or send a challenge. You are supposed to be cool and collected, and your friend's feelings are more or less irritated.

2. Use every effort to soothe and tranquilize your principal; do not see things in the same aggravated light in which he views them; extenuate the conduct of his adversary whenever you see clearly an opportunity to do so, without doing violence to your friend's irritated mind. Endeavor to persuade him that there must have been some misunderstanding in the matter. Check him if he uses opprobrious epithets towards his adversary, and never permit improper or insulting words in the note you carry.

3. To the note you carry in writing to the party complained of, you are entitled to a written answer, which will be directed to your principal, and will be delivered to

you by his adversary's friend. If this note be not written in the style of a gentleman, refuse to receive it, and assign your reason for such refusal. If there be a question made as to the character of the note, require the second presenting it to you, who considers it respectful, to endorse upon it these words: "I consider the note of my friend respectful, and would not have been the bearer of it, if I believed otherwise."

4. If the party called on, refuses to receive the note you bear, you are entitled to demand a reason for such refusal. If he refuses to give you any reason, and persists in such refusal, he treats not only your friend, but yourself, with indignity, and you must then make yourself the actor by sending a respectful note, requiring a proper explanation of the course he has pursued towards you and your friend, and if he still adheres to his determination, you are to challenge or post him.

5. If the person to whom you deliver the note of your friend, declines meeting him on the ground of inequality, you are bound to tender yourself in his stead, by a note directed to him from yourself, and if he refuse to meet you, you are to post him.

6. In all cases of the substitution of the second for the principal, the second should interpose and adjust the matter, if the party substituting avows he does not make the quarrel of his principal his own. The true reason of substitution is, the supposed insult of imputing to you the like inequality which is charged upon your friend; and when the contrary is declared, there should be no fight, for individuals may well differ in their estimate of an individual's character and standing in society. In case of substitution and a satisfactory arrangement, you are then to inform your friend of all the facts, whose duty it will be to post in person.

7. If the party, to whom you present a note, employ a

son, father, or brother, as a second, you must decline acting with either, on the ground of consanguinity.

8. If a minor wishes you to take a note to an adult, decline doing so on the ground of his minority. But if the adult complained of, had made a companion of the minor in society, you may bear the note.

9. When an accommodation is tendered, never require too much; and if the party offering the *amende* honorable wishes to give a reason for his conduct in the matter, do not, unless offensive to your friend, refuse to receive it; by so doing, you heal the breach the more effectually.

10. If a stranger wish you to bear a note for him, be well satisfied, before you do so, that he is on an equality with you; and in presenting the note, state to the party the relationship you stand towards him, and what you know and believe about him; for strangers are entitled to redress for wrongs as well as others, and the rules of honor and hospitality should protect them.

CHAPTER II.

THE PARTY RECEIVING A NOTE BEFORE CHALLENGE.

1. When a note is presented to you by an equal, receive it, and read it, although you may suppose it to be from one you do not intend to meet, because its requisites may be of a character which may be readily complied with. But if the requirements of the note cannot be acceded to, return it through the medium of your friend to the person who handed it to you, with your reason for returning it.

2. If the note received be in abusive terms, object to its reception, and return it for that reason, but if it be respectful, return an answer of the same character, in which respond correctly and openly to all interrogatories fairly pro-

pounded, and hand it to your friend, whom, it is presumed, you have consulted, and who has advised the answer, directed to the opposite party, and let it be delivered to his friend.

3. You may refuse to receive a note from a minor, if you have not made an associate of him; one that has been posted; one that has been publicly disgraced without resenting it; one whose occupation is unlawful; a man in his dotage and a lunatic. There may be other cases, but the character of those enumerated will lead to a correct decision upon those aomitted.

If you receive a note from a stranger, you have a right to a reasonable time to ascertain his standing in society, unless he be fully vouched for by his friend.

4. If a party delays calling on you for a week or more after the supposed insult, and assigns no cause for the delay, if you require it, you may double the time before you respond to him; for the wrong cannot be considered aggravated if borne patiently for some days, and the time may have been used in preparation and practice.

SECOND'S DUTY OF THE PARTY RECEIVING A NOTE BEFORE CHALLENGE SENT.

1. When consulted by your friend who has received a note, requiring explanation, inform him distinctly that he must be governed wholly by you in the progress of the dispute. If he refuses, decline to act on that ground.

2. Use your utmost efforts to allay all excitement which your principal may labor under; search diligently into the origin of the misunderstanding, for gentlemen seldom insult each other, unless they labor under some misapprehension or mistake; and when you have discovered the original ground of error, follow each movement to the time of sending the note, and harmony will be restored.

3. When your principal refuses to do what you require of him, decline further acting, on that ground, and inform the opposing second of your withdrawal from the negotiation.

CHAPTER III.

DUTY OF CHALLENGEE AND HIS SECOND BEFORE FIGHTING.

1. After all efforts for a reconciliation are over, the party aggrieved sends a challenge to his adversary, which is delivered to his second.

2. Upon the acceptance of the challenge, the seconds make the necessary arrangements for the meeting, in which each party is entitled to a perfect equality. The old notion that the party challenged was authorized to name the time, place, distance and weapon, has been long since exploded, nor would a man of chivalric honor use such a right if he possessed it. The time must be as soon as practicable, the place such as had ordinarily been used where the parties are, the distance usual, and the weapon that which is most generally used, which in this State is the pistol.

3. If the challengee insist upon what is not usual in time, place, distance and weapon, do not yield the point, and tender in writing what is usual in each, and if he refuse to give satisfaction, then your friend may post him.

4. If your friend be determined to fight and not post, you have the right to withdraw. But if you continue to act, and the challengee name a distance and weapon not usual, and more fatal than the ordinary distance and weapon, you have the right to tender a still more deadly distance and weapon, and he must accept.

5. The usual distance is from ten to twenty paces, as

may be agreed on, and the seconds in measuring the ground usually step three feet.

6. After all the arrangements are made, the seconds determine the giving of the word and position by lot, and he who gains has the choice of the one or the other, selects whether it be the word or position, but he cannot have both.

CHAPTER IV.

DUTY OF CHALLENGEE AND SECOND AFTER CHALLENGE SENT.

1. The challengee has no option when negotiation has ceased but to accept the challenge.

2. The second makes the necessary arrangements with the second of the person challenging. The arrangements are detailed in the preceding chapter.

CHAPTER V.

DUTIES OF PRINCIPALS AND SECONDS ON THE GROUND.

1. The principals are to be respectful in meeting, and neither by look nor expression irritate each other. They are to be wholly passive, being entirely under the guidance of the seconds.

2. When once posted they are not to quit their positions under any circumstances, without the leave or direction of their second.

3. When the principals are posted, the second giving the word must tell them to stand firm until he repeats the giving of the word, in the manner it will be given, when the parties are at liberty to fire.

4. Each second has a loaded pistol, in order to enforce a

fair combat according to the rules agreed on; and if a principal fires before the word or time agreed on, he is at liberty to fire at him, and if such second's principal fall, it is his duty to do so.

5. If, after a fire, either party be touched, the duel is to end, and no second is excusable who permits a wounded friend to fight; nor no second who knows his duty will permit his friend to fight a man already hit. I am aware there have been many instances where a contest has continued, not only after slight, but severe wounds had been received. In all such cases I think the seconds are blamable.

6. If, after an exchange of shots, neither party is hit, it is the duty of the second of the challengee to approach the second of the challenger and say: "Our friends have exchanged shots, are you satisfied, or is there any cause why the contest should be continued?" If the meeting be of no serious cause of complaint, where the party complaining had in no way been deeply injured, or grossly insulted, the second of the party challenging should reply: "The point of honor being settled, there can, I conceive, be no objection to a reconciliation, and I propose that our principals meet on middle ground, shake hands, and be friends." If this be acceded to by the second of the challengee, the second of the party challenging will say, "We have agreed that the present duel shall cease, the honor of each of you is preserved, and you will meet on middle ground, shake hands, and be reconciled."

7. If the insult be of a serious character, it will be the duty of the second of the challenger to say, in reply to the second of the challengee, "We have been deeply wronged, and if you are not disposed to repair the injury, the contest must continue." And if the second of the challengee offers nothing by way of reparation, the fight continues until one or the other of the principals is hit.

8. If, in cases where the contest is ended by the seconds, as mentioned in the sixth rule of this chapter, the parties refuse to meet and be reconciled, it is the duty of the seconds to withdraw from the field, informing their principals that the contest must be continued under the superintendence of other friends. But if one agrees to this arrangement of the seconds, and the other does not, the second of the disagreeing principal only withdraws.

9. If either principal on the ground, refuse to fight, or continue the fight when required, it is the duty of his second to say to the other second, "I have come upon the ground with a coward, and have to tender you my apology for an ignorance of his character; you are at liberty to post him." The second by such conduct stands excused to the opposite party.

10. When the duel is ended by a party being hit, it is the duty of the second to the party so hit, to announce the fact to the second of the party hitting, who will forthwith tender any assistance he can command to the disabled principal. If the party challenging hit the challengee, it is his duty to say he is satisfied, and will leave the ground. If the challenger be hit, upon the challengee being informed of it, he should ask, through his second, whether he was at liberty to leave the ground, which should be assented to.

CHAPTER VI.

WHO SHOULD BE ON THE GROUND.

1. The principals, seconds, and one surgeon and one assistant surgeon to each principal; but the assistant surgeon may be dispensed with.

2. Any number of friends that the seconds agree on may

be present, provided they do not come within the degrees of consanguinity mentioned in the seventh rule of Chapter I.

3. Persons admitted on the ground are carefully to abstain, by word or behavior, from any act that might be the least exceptionable; nor should they stand near the principals or seconds, or hold conversations with them.

CHAPTER VII.

ARMS, AND MANNER OF LOADING AND PRESENTING THEM.

1. THE arms used should be smooth-bore pistols, not exceeding nine inches in length, with flint and steel. Percussion pistols may be mutually used if agreed on, but to object on that account is lawful.

2. Each second informs the other when he is about to load, and invites his presence, but the second rarely attends on such invitation, as gentlemen may be safely trusted in the matter.

3. The second in presenting the pistol to his friend should never put it in the pistol hand, but should place it in the other, which is grasped midway the barrel, with the muzzle pointing in the contrary way to that which he is to fire, informing him that his pistol is loaded and ready for use. Before the word is given the principal grasps the butt firmly in his pistol hand, and brings it round, with the muzzle downward, to the fighting position.

4. The fighting position is with the muzzle down, and the barrel from you; for although it may be agreed that you may hold your pistols with the muzzle up, it may be objected to, as you can fire sooner from that position, and consequently have a decided advantage, which ought not to be claimed, and should not be granted.

CHAPTER VIII.

THE DEGREES OF INSULT, AND HOW COMPROMISED.

1. THE prevailing rule is that words used in retort, although more violent and disrespectful than those first used, will not satisfy, words being no satisfaction for words.

2. When words are used, and a blow given in return, the insult is avenged, and if redress is sought, it must be from the person receiving the blow.

3. When blows are given in the first instance and returned, and the person first striking be badly beaten or otherwise, the party first struck is to make the demand, for blows do not satisfy a blow.

4. Insults at the wine-table, when the company are over-excited, must be answered for; and, if the party insulting have no recollection of the insult, it is his duty to say so in writing and negative the insult. For instance, if a man say, "You are a liar and no gentleman," he must, in addition to the plea of want of recollection, say, "I believe the party insulted to be a man of the strictest veracity and a gentleman."

5. Intoxication is not a full excuse for insult, but it will greatly palliate. If it was a full excuse, it might well be counterfeited to wound feelings, or destroy character.

6. In all cases of intoxication the seconds must use a sound discretion under the above general rules.

7. Can every insult be compromised, is a moot and vexed question. On this subject no rules can be given that will be satisfactory. The old opinion, that a blow must require blood, is not of force. Blows may be compromised in many cases. What those cases are, must depend on the seconds.

CODE OF DUELING ESTABLISHED IN FRANCE.

COPIED FROM MILLINGEN'S "HISTORY OF DUELING."

THE French admit three sorts of offences:

First. A simple offence.

Second. An offence of an insulting nature.

Third. An offence with personal acts of violence. In these cases they have established the following rules, which, indeed, so long as dueling is tolerated, may be considered most judicious, and such as should regulate the arrangement of all quarrels.

Rule 1. If, in the course of a discussion, an offence is offered, the person who has been offended is the injured party. If this injury is followed by a blow, unquestionably the party that has been struck is the injured one. To return one blow by another of a more serious nature—severely wounding, for instance, after a slap in the face—does not constitute the person who received the second blow, however severe it may have been, the party originally insulted. In this case, satisfaction may be demanded by the party that was first struck. Such a case must be referred to the chances of a meeting.

Rule 2. If an insult follows an unpolite expression—if the aggressor considers himself offended, or if the person who has received the insult, considers himself insulted—the case must also be referred to a meeting.

Rule 3. If, in the course of a discussion, during which the rules of politeness have not been transgressed, but in consequence of which, expressions have been made use of which induce one of the party to consider himself offended, the man who demands satisfaction cannot be considered the aggressor, or the person who gives it the offender. This case must be submitted to the trial of chance.

Rule 4. But if a man sends a message without a sufficient cause, in this case he becomes the aggressor; and the seconds, before they allow a meeting to take place, must insist upon a sufficient reason being manifestly shown.

Rule 5. A son may espouse the cause of his father, if he is too aged to resent an insult, or if the age of the aggressor is of great disparity; but a son cannot espouse the quarrel of his father if he has been the aggressor.

Rule 6. There are offences of such a galling nature, that they may lead the insulted party to have recourse to acts of violence. Such acts ought invariably to be avoided, as they can only tend to mortal combat.

Rule 7. The offended party has the choice of arms.*

Rule 8. When the offence has been of a degrading nature, the offended has the right to name both the arms and the duel.†

Rule 9. When the offence has been attended by acts of violence, the offended party has the right to name his duel, his arms, the distance, and may insist upon the aggressor not using his own arms, to which he may have become accustomed by practice; but in this case the offended party must also use weapons in which he is not practised.

Rule 10. There are only three legal arms; the sword, the saber, the pistol. The saber may be refused even by the aggressor, especially if he is a retired officer; but it may be always objected to by a civilian.

Rule 11. When a challenge is sent, or a meeting demanded, the parties have a mutual right to the name and address of each other.

---

* This is a point of such vital importance, that it is impossible to be too careful in ascertaining, coolly and deliberately, from which of the parties the insult originated.

† To name a duel, refers to time and place.

Rule 12. The parties should immediately after seek their seconds, sending to each other the names and addresses of their seconds.*

Rule 13. Honor can never be compromised by the offending party admitting that they were in the wrong.

If the apology of the offending party is deemed sufficient by the seconds of the offended; if the seconds express their satisfaction, and are ready to affirm this opinion in writing; or if the offender has tendered a written apology, considered of a satisfactory nature; in such a case the party that offers to apologize ceases to be the offender; and if his adversary persists, the arms must be decided by drawing lots. However, no apology can be received after a blow. An amicable arrangement of a quarrel should take place before the parties meet on the ground, unless circumstances prevent a prior interview. Howbeit, if when upon the ground, and even when armed, one of the parties thinks proper to apologize, and the seconds of the offended party are satisfied, it is only the party that tenders the apology upon whom any future unfavorable reflections can be cast.

Rule 14. If the seconds of the offending party come to the ground with an apology, instead of bringing forward their principal, it is only to them that blame can be attached, as the honor of their principal was placed in their hands.

Rule 15. No challenge can be sent by collective parties. If any body or society of men have received an insult, they can only send an individual belonging to it, to demand

* This is a point of great importance. It sometimes happens that a man who has insulted another will select as his second some notorious ruffian, who will, to use the common expression, "fix a quarrel" on him, and endeavor to fight for his principal. Not long ago a fellow advertised himself in the public papers to fight for any person who might require his services.—*Millingen.*

satisfaction. A message collectively sent may be refused; but the challenged party may select an antagonist, or leave the nomination to chance.

Rule 16. All duels should take place during the forty-eight hours that have succeeded the offence, unless it is otherwise stipulated by the seconds.*

Rule 17. In a duel with pistol or saber, two seconds to each combatant are indispensable; one will suffice when the sword is used.

Rule 18. It is the duty of the seconds to decide upon the necessity of the duel, and to state their opinions to their principals. After having consulted with them in such a manner as not to allow any chance of avoiding a duel to escape, they must again meet, and exert their best endeavors to settle the business amicably. If they fail in this attempt, they must then decide upon arms, time, place, distance, and mode of fighting; and at the same time they must endeavor to come to some arrangement regarding any difficulties that might arise, when the parties are on the ground.

Rule 19. Seconds are not witnesses; and each second should have a witness.

Rule 20. No second or witness shall become a principal on the spot. Any insult received by them constitutes a fresh offence.

Rule 21. The seconds should not remain more than ten minutes on the ground without a combat.

Rule 22. The seconds in a duel with swords, may request that the offended party shall be allowed to ward off a lunge with the left hand. This, however, may be refused by the seconds of the aggressor.

---

* This rule is of importance. Forty-eight hours may be considered a fair time to reflect upon the painful necessity of a hostile meeting; and there is, in general, reason to suppose that a challenge, sent long after a provocation, has been the result of the interference of busy friends.—*Millingen.*

Rule 23. The seconds of the aggressor may, if they think proper, refuse to fire by signal, if the aggressor had not struck his antagonist.

Rule 24. The seconds must determine whether the combatants in sword duels shall be allowed to take breath.

Rule 25. The seconds will also decide (without acquainting their principals of this decision), whether the parties are to be separated after the first wound. In this arrangement they will be guided by the nature of the quarrel.

Rule 26. They will also decide whether a fencing-glove, or any other article to wrap round the hand, is to be allowed; a string,* or common glove, are always allowed.

Rule 27. The seconds are never to let their principals know that they are of opinion that the nature of the insult received is such as to render a mortal combat necessary.

Rule 28. The seconds may refuse the sword, if the principal is unable to use it from any infirmity, unless the offended party has received a personal injury.

Rule 29. The second of a person blind of one eye, may object to the pistol, unless the aggressor has struck him.

Rule 30. The sword or saber may be declined by the seconds of a person with only one leg or arm.

Rule 31. The seconds of a young man shall not allow him to fight an adversary above sixty years of age, unless this adversary had struck him; and in this case his challenge must be accepted in writing. His refusal to comply with this rule is tantamount to a refusal to give satisfaction, and the young man's honor is thereby satisfied.

Rule 32. If any unfair occurrence takes place in a duel, it is the duty of the seconds to commit the circumstance to paper, and follow it up before the competent tribunals, *when they are bound in honor to give true evidence.*

Rule 33. It is the duty of seconds to separate the com-

* Sword-knot.

batants the very moment that the stipulated rules are transgressed.

Rule 34. A father, a brother, a son, or any relative in the first degree, cannot serve as a second for or against his relative.

Rule 35. In sword duels the seconds will mark the standing-spot of each combatant, leaving a distance of two feet between the points of their weapons. The standing-ground to be drawn for by lots.

Rule 36. The swords must be measured to ascertain that they are of equal length; in no instance must a sword with a sharp edge or a notch be allowed.

Rule 37. The combatants will be requested to throw off their coats, and to lay bare their breasts, to show that they do not wear any defence that could ward off a thrust. A refusal to submit to this proposal is to be considered a refusal to fight.

Rule 38. The offended party can always use his own weapons, if they are considered of a description fitting the combat. If, on comparing arms, the swords should be found to differ, the choice must be decided by chance, unless the disproportion is of a material nature.

Rule 39. When the hand is wrapped up in a handkerchief, an end of it is not allowed to hang down. Should the party refuse to draw it up, the seconds may insist that he throws it off altogether, and is only allowed a sword-knot. If fencing-gloves are allowed, and one party declines their use, the other is not to be deprived of them; but if only one glove has been brought to the ground, it cannot be used.

Rule 40. When the combatants are on the ground, the seconds are to explain to them all the stipulated arrangements, that they may not deviate from them on plea of ignorance. This being done, the signal of attack is given in the word "Go" (*allez*); but if before this signal the parties have already crossed swords, the signal is not necessary; but the first who advanced without it is liable to censure.

Rule 41. The seconds shall hold a sword or a cane, bearing the point downward, and, standing close to each combatant, be prepared to stop the combat the moment that the rules agreed upon are transgressed.

Rule 42. Unless previously stipulated, neither of the combatants shall be allowed to turn off the sword of his adversary with the left hand; should a combatant persist in thus using his left hand, the seconds of his adversary may insist that the hand shall be confined behind his back.

Rule 43. In a sword duel the combatants are allowed to raise themselves, to stoop, to vault to the right or to the left, and turn round each other.

Rule 44. When one of the combatants exclaims that he is wounded, or a wound is perceived by his second, the combat is to be stopped. With the consent of the wounded man the combat may be renewed.

Rule 45. If the wounded man, although the combat is ordered to be stopped, shall continue to press upon his adversary with precipitation; this act is tantamount to his desire to continue the conflict, but he must be stopped and reprimanded. If, under similar circumstances, the combatant that is not wounded continues to press on his antagonist, although ordered to stop by the seconds, he must be immediately checked by them, and considered as having infringed the stipulated rules.

Rule 46. When a second raises his sword or cane, it must be considered as the signal to stop; in such cases, the other second shall cry out "stop," when the parties must recede one step, still remaining in guard.

Rule 47. In pistol duels, the nearest distance should be fifteen paces. The sight of the pistol should be fixed, and not more than fifteen lines difference be allowed in the length of the barrel. It is also desirable that the barrel should not be rifled, and that the pistols should be of a similar description.

Rule 48. The stand of each combatant to be decided by lot.

Rule 49. It is desirable that the same pair of pistols be used by both parties.

Rule 50. The seconds shall load the pistol with most scrupulous care, and in the presence of each other. If one pair of pistols is used, each second will use a similar charge, by allowing the other to try the charge with a ramrod, or by loading in the presence of four witnesses.*

Rule 51. Tho combatants must be placed on the ground by their respective seconds; if thirty-five paces have been fixed upon, the offended party has the right to the first fire; if only fifteen paces are marked, the first fire must be decided by drawing lots.

Rule 52. The seconds have a right to ascertain that the principals do not carry any defense about their persons. A refusal to submit to this examination is to be considered as a refusal to fight.

Rule 53. The seconds of both parties shall stand together; having taken their ground, they first command, "Make ready," which is followed by the word "Fire."

Rule 54. A miss-fire is considered a shot, unless stipulation to the contrary has been made.

Rule 55. If one of the party is wounded, he may fire upon his antagonist, but not after the expiration of two minutes.

Rule 56. When both parties have fired without effect, the pistols are to be re-loaded, in the same manner as before.

---

* "The trial by ramrod is an uncertain mode, as the depth of the charge will vary according to the wadding; a regular powder measure is the only method that canse cure a fair proceeding," etc.—*Millingen.*

Rule 57. In the pistol duel *à volonté*, the seconds are to mark out the ground, at a distance of thirty-five to forty paces; two lines are then to be traced between these two distances, leaving an interval of from twenty to fifteen paces, thus each combatant can advance ten paces.

Rule 58. The ground being taken, one of the seconds, drawn by lot, gives the word, "March."

Rule 59. The combatants then advance upon each other, if they think proper, holding their pistols vertically while advancing; but they may level the weapons and take aim on halting, although they may not fire at the time, but continue to march on unto the line of separation, marked with a cane, or a handkerchief, where they must stop and fire. But, although one of the parties may thus advance to the limits, his antagonist is not obliged to move on, whether he has received the fire of his antagonist, or reserved his own.

Rule 60. The moment one of the combatants has fired, he must halt upon the spot, and stand firmly, to receive the fire of his adversary, who is not, however, allowed more than one minute to advance and fire, or to fire from the ground he stands on.

Rule 61. The wounded party is allowed one minute to fire upon his antagonist, from the moment he is hit; but if he has fallen on the ground, he will be allowed two minutes to recover.

Rule 62. In this form of duel, a pair of pistols may be allowed each combatant; but this is only allowed when one of the parties has received a blow. In these cases, a pistol of a different pair is to be given to each combatant. The affair cannot be considered terminated, unless the four pistols have been discharged.

Rule 63. When four pistols are used, if one of the party is wounded, the contest must cease, and the wounded man not be allowed to fire, as it is evident that his antagonist, who might remain with a loaded pistol, would have an unfair advantage over him, in a cool, deliberate fire.

Rule 64. When one of the parties is wounded, the affair must be considered ended, even though the wounded party should express his wish to proceed, unless the seconds consider him in a fit state to continue the combat.

Rule 65. In the pistol duel called *à marche interrompre*, a distance of forty-five or fifty paces is measured, and two lines are traced and marked between the distance of fifteen to twenty paces; thus the combatants may advance fifteen paces.

Rule 66. On the word "*March*," the combatants may advance in a zigzag step, not exceeding two paces. They may take aim without firing, and, while advancing, stop when they choose, and advance again; but once having fired, both parties must halt on the spot.

Rule 67. The combatant who has not fired may now fire, but without advancing, and the party who has fired must firmly stand the fire of his antagonist, who for that purpose is allowed half a minute; if he allows a longer time to elapse, he must be disarmed by the seconds.

Rule 68. In the pistol duel called *à ligne parallèle*, two parallel lines are traced by the seconds, fifteen paces from each other, and from thirty-five to twenty-five paces in length.

Rule 69. The combatants are placed at the extremity of each line, fronting each other.

Rule 70. The seconds stand behind their principals, in a situation that may not expose them to the fire of the parties. The signal is given by the word "*March.*"

Rule 71. The combatants then advance, not upon each other, but in the direction of the line that has been traced for them; and therefore, whether one of the adversaries has advanced or not, he will find himself placed fifteen paces from the other.

Rule 72. The champion who fires must stop; but he may halt without firing, take aim, and continue to advance.

Rule 73. In the pistol duel called *au signal*, the signal is to be given by the second of the offended party, by three claps on the hand, three seconds being counted between each clap, which will take up nine seconds; or two seconds which will take up six seconds. In other cases the seconds draw lots for giving the signal.

Rule 74. The combatants, when they have received their arms, are to walk, but to keep the muzzles of their pistols pointing to the ground; at the first signal they will raise their arms, take aim at the second signal, and fire simultaneously at the third.

Rule 75. If one of the combatants fires before the third signal, or half a second after it, he is to be considered as a dishonorable man, and, if his antagonist is killed, an assassin. And if he fires before the signal without effect, his opponent has a right to take as much time as he thinks proper, to level at him and shoot him.

Rule 76. If one of the parties has fired agreeably to the stipulated signal, and his antagonist has dishonorably reserved his fire, it is the duty of the seconds, at all risk and peril, to rush upon him and disarm him. In this case, the party who has observed the rules, has a right to demand another duel of a different form.

Rule 77. The second who is to give the signal, should warn the combatants of the nature of the signal, in a loud and audible voice, in the following words: "Recollect, gentlemen, that honor demands that you should only fire upon the third signal being given; that you are not to raise your arm until the first signal, and not to fire until the third. I am now going to give the signals, which will consist of three claps on the hand."

Rule 78. In the duel with sabers, the seconds should endeavor to have it fought with short sabers, these arms being less fatal than long ones.

Rule 79. The ground taken, the antagonists are to be placed opposite each other, at the distance of one foot from their saber points.

Rule 80. In general these duels are fought with cuff-gloves; but, otherwise, the parties may wrap a handkerchief round their hand and wrist, provided that no end is allowed to hang down.

Rule 81. In regiments, the regimental saber is to be the one selected, provided that they are of the same length, and mounted in the same manner. The same precautionary steps are to be adopted as in the sword duel, to ascertain that no defence is worn by either party.

Rule 82. The signal of "*Allez,*" "Go," having been given, the combatants advance upon each other, and either give point or cut; vaulting, advancing, or retreating at pleasure.

Rule 83. To strike an adversary when disarmed, to seize his arm, his body, or his weapon, is a foul proceeding. A combatant is disarmed when his saber is either wrenched from him or dropped.

Rule 84. In *saber* duels in which the point of the arm is not to be used, sabers without a point are to be chosen. To give point and kill an adversary by the infringement of this rule, is to be considered an assassination. These duels should always be considered as terminated on the first loss of blood.

The preceding rules, which are founded upon long experience, in this fatal practice, have been sanctioned by twenty-five general officers, eleven peers of France, and fifty officers of rank. The Minister of War, who could not, consistently with his public duties, affix his signature to the document, gave his approbation in an official letter, and the majority of the prefects equally sanctioned the regulation.

IRISH CODE.

AS GIVEN BY SIR JONAH BARRINGTON, IN PERSONAL SKETCHES OF HIS OWN TIME.

RULES OF DUELING.

THE practice of dueling and points of honor settled at Clonmell Summer Assizes, 1877, by the gentlemen delegates of Tipperary, Galway, Mayo, Sligo, and Roscommon, and prescribed for general adoption throughout Ireland.

Rule 1. The first offence requires the first apology, though the retort may have been more offensive than the insult. Example: A tells B he is impertinent, etc.; B retorts that he lies—yet, A must make the first apology, because he gave the first offence; and then (after one fire) B may explain away the retort by subsequent apology.

Rule 2. But if the parties would rather fight on, then, after two shots each (but in no case before), B may explain first, and A apologize afterwards.

N. B.—The above rules apply to all cases of offences in retort, not of a stronger class than the example.

Rule 3. If a doubt exist who gave the first offence, the decision rests with the seconds; if they *won't* decide, or *can't* agree, the matter must proceed to two shots, or to a hit, if the challenger require it.

Rule 4. When the *lie direct* is the *first* offence, the aggressor must either beg pardon in express terms, exchange two shots previous to apology, or three shots, followed by explanation; or fire on until a severe hit be received by one party or the other.

Rule 5. As a blow is strictly prohibited under any circumstances amongst gentlemen, no verbal apology can be received for such an insult; the alternatives therefore are—the offender handing a cane to the injured party, to be used on his own back, at the same time begging pardon; firing on until one, or both, is disabled; or exchanging three shots, and then asking pardon, *without* the proffer of the cane.

If swords are used, the parties engage till one is well blooded, disabled, or disarmed; or until, after receiving a wound, and blood being drawn, the aggressor begs pardon.

N. B.—A *disarm* is considered the same as a *disable;* the disarmer may (strictly) break his adversary's sword; but if it be the challenger who is disarmed, it is considered ungenerous to do so.

In case the challenged be disarmed, and refuses to ask pardon, or atone, he must not be *killed,* as formerly, but the challenger may lay his own sword on the aggressor's shoulder, then break the aggressor's sword, and say, "I spare your life!" The challenged can never revive that quarrel—the challenger may.

Rule 6. If A gives B the lie, and B retorts by a blow (being the two greatest offences), no reconciliation *can* take place, till after two discharges each, or a severe hit, *after* which B may beg A's pardon humbly for the blow, and then A may explain simply for the lie; because a blow is *never* allowable, and the offence of the lie, therefore, merges in it. (See preceding rule.)

N. B.—Challenges for undivulged causes may be reconciled on the ground, after one shot. An explanation, or the slightest hit, should be sufficient in such cases, because no personal offence transpired.

Rule 7. But no apology can be received in any case after the parties have actually taken their ground, without exchange of fires.

Rule 8. In the above case, no challenger is obliged to divulge his cause of challenge (if private), unless required by the challenged so to do *before* their meeting.

Rule 9. All imputations of cheating at play, races, etc., to be considered equivalent to a blow, but may be reconciled after one shot, on admitting their falsehood, and begging pardon publicly.

Rule 10. Any insult to a lady under a gentleman's care or protection, to be considered as, by one degree, a greater offence than if given to the gentleman personally, and to be regulated accordingly.

Rule 11. Offences originating or accruing from the support of ladies' reputation, to be considered as less unjustifiable than any others of the same class, and as admitting of slighter apologies by the aggressor, this to be determined by the circumstances of the case, but *always* favorably to the lady.

Rule 12. In simple unpremeditated *rencontres* with the small sword, or *couteau-de-chasse,* the rule is—first draw, first sheathe; unless blood be drawn; then both sheathe and proceed to investigation.

Rule 13. No dumb shooting or firing in the air admissible *in any case.* The challenger ought not to have challenged without receiving offence; and the challenged ought, if he gave offence, to have made an apology before he came on the ground; therefore, *children's play* must be dishonorable on one side or the other, and is accordingly prohibited.

Rule 14. Seconds to be of equal rank in society with the principals they attend, inasmuch as a second may either choose or chance to become a principal, and *equality is indispensable.*

Rule 15. Challenges are never to be delivered at night, unless the party to be challenged intend leaving the place of offence before morning; for it is desirable to avoid all hot-headed proceedings.

Rule 16. The challenged has the right to choose his own weapon, unless the challenger gives his honor he is no swordsman; after which, however, he cannot decline any *second* species of weapon proposed by the challenger.

Rule 17. The challenged chooses his ground; the challenger chooses his distance; the seconds fix the time and terms of firing.

Rule 18. The seconds load in presence of each other, unless they give their mutual honors they have charged smooth and single, which should be held sufficient.

Rule 19. Firing may be regulated—first, by signal; secondly, by word of command; or, thirdly, at pleasure—as may be agreeable to the parties. In the latter case the parties may fire at their reasonable leisure, but *second presents* and *rests* are strictly prohibited.

Rule 20. In all cases, a miss-fire is equivalent to a shot, and a *snap* or a *non-cock* is to be considered as a miss-fire.

Rule 21. Seconds are bound to attempt a reconciliation *before* the meeting takes place, or *after* sufficient firing or hits, as specified.

Rule 22. Any wound sufficient to agitate the nerves, and necessarily make the hand shake, must end the business for *that day*.

Rule 23. If the cause of meeting be of such a nature that no apology or explanation can or will be received, the challenged takes his ground, and calls on the challenger to proceed as he chooses; in such cases, firing at pleasure is the usual practice, but may be varied by agreement.

Rule 24. In slight cases the second hands his principal but one pistol; but in gross cases two, holding another case ready charged in reserve.

Rule 25. Where seconds disagree and resolve to exchange shots themselves, it must be at the same time, and at right angles with their principals, thus:

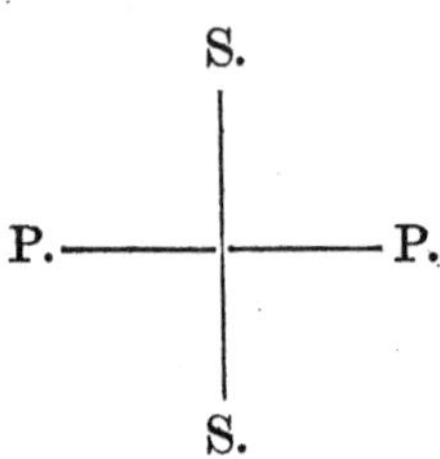

If with swords, side by side, with five paces interval.

N. B.—All matters and doubts not herein mentioned, will be explained and cleared up by application to the committee, who meet alternately at Clonmell and Galway, at the Quarter Sessions, for that purpose.

Crow Ryan, *President.*
James Keogh, } *Secretaries.*
Amby Bodkin, }

ADDITIONAL GALWAY ARTICLES.

Rule 1. No party can be allowed to bend his knee or cover his side with his left hand; but may present at any level from the hip to the eye.

Rule 2. None can either advance or retreat, if the ground be measured; if no ground be measured, either party may advance at his pleasure, even to touch muzzles; but neither can advance on his adversary after the fire, unless the adversary steps forward on him.

N. B.—The seconds on both sides stand responsible for this last rule being *strictly* observed; bad cases having accrued from neglecting of it.

When the above code was issued, it was directed that all gentlemen throughout the kingdom should observe it, and keep a copy always in their pistol-cases, that ignorance might never be pleaded.

CERTIFICATES.

No. 1.

Oath of Caroline Myers, charging paternity of her illegitimate child to Thomas K. Smith. Sworn to before Peter Carson, Justice of the Peace, 7th of October, 1871. Certified to by F. H. Buford, Clerk Circuit Court, Bibb County, Alabama.

No. 2.

Major Woodson:—At your request, I state what I know of the Smith-Myers bastardy case. I was an attorney engaged to prosecute Thomas K. Smith, and had in my possession several letters written by him to her, advising the taking the life of the child, and the swearing of it first to one and then to another gentleman in the city. Upon the settlement of the case, Mr. Smith admitted to me his criminal intimacy with prosecutrix, and that the letters aforesaid had been written by him.

Charles Ford.

No. 3.

I was formerly a partner of Thomas K. Smith, and he frequently mentioned to me his criminal intimacy with Caroline Myers, detailing circumstances.

William Hart.

No. 4.

I certify that three months before the birth of the child, Thomas K. Smith came to me and stated that he had frequent criminal connection with Miss Caroline Myers, and that he expected a prosecution, and employed me to defend him; that he had advised her to swear the paternity of the child to a gentleman living in the city, but she had refused to do so.

George M. Gulp,
Attorney-at-Law.

www.ingramcontent.com/pod-product-compliance
Lightning Source LLC
LaVergne TN
LVHW010216110826
845151LV00004B/1097